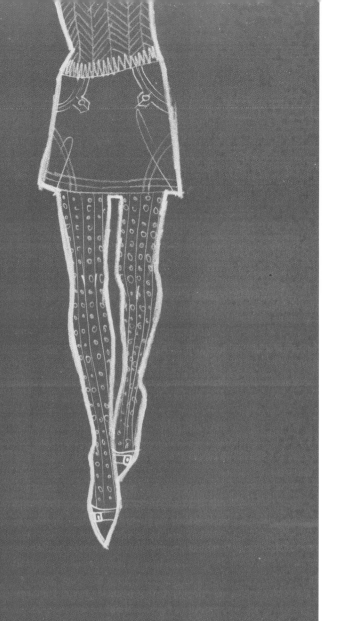

CONTENTS

HOW TO DRAW

ILLUSTRATION TECHNIQUES

INTRODUCTION

I have a passion for drawing. I have been teaching fashion illustration classes for several years and I enjoy transmitting my knowledge and providing my students with the keys that can help them resolve the doubts that can appear when studying a practical subject such as this one.

Since the market offered no book that was adequate for learning purposes, I gradually compiled my own manual to give my classes, with notes that contain illustrations in various techniques, sketches of the body and body parts, comprehension exercises, and some tricks of the trade and advice.

Then, one day Loft Publications called me at my studio with a fabulous request: design a book, aimed at teaching and for consulting, to initiate the reader in the drawing of fashion illustration. A real challenge!

I immediately set to work and started by writing out all my notes using a wider and more detailed language. So much material had accumulated that I decided to divide it into two big sections: *How to Draw* and *Illustration Techniques*. I then looked for

help. This was easy. There were none better then two great illustrators and friends of mine, Javier Navarro and Juanjo Navarro, who, by the way, are not related. And from then on it was all draw, draw, and draw. Always with the same imposition: not a single drawing was done with a computer, they were all drawn freehand.

The final result is a piece of work whose aim is to submerge the reader in the world of illustration. True to the clarity of the reasons that lie behind it, the content is also clearly presented. The first section ranges from how to start drawing a human figure to the techniques to stylize and synthesize it. This section provides a large amount of figures in different poses, as well as hands and feet—often the most difficult parts—in diverse postures and angles. However, in the field of fashion illustration it is also essential to know how to draw fabric, and even more important to know how to draw the folds of clothing. The items of clothing are presented as much in technical drawing as in figures in movement, and forming light and shadow is also explained, as this gives quality to the illustration.

Essential FASHION Illustration

GLOUCESTER MASSACHUSETTS

ROCKPORT
PUBLISHERS

ESSENTIAL FASHION ILLUSTRATION
Copyright © 2005 by LOFT Publications

First published in the United States of America by
Rockport Publishers, a member of
Quayside Publishing Group
33 Commercial Street
Gloucester, MA 01930-0589
Telephone: (978) 282-9590
Fax: (978) 283-2742
www.rockpub.com

ISBN-13: 978-1-59253-253-7
ISBN-10: 1-59253-253-5

Publisher:
Paco Asensio

Concept:
Maite Lafuente

Illustrations:
Maite Lafuente
Javier Navarro
Juanjo Navarro

Translation:
Jay Noden

Art Director:
Mireia Casanovas Soley

Graphic Design and Layout:
Cris Tarradas Dulcet

Editorial project:
2005 © LOFT Publications
Via Laietana 32, 4th Of. 92.
08003 Barcelona. Spain
Tel.: +34 932 688 088
Fax: +34 932 687 073
loft@loftpublications.com
www.loftpublications.com

Printed in China

The second part of the book revolves around color and the different techniques with which one can work: watercolor, wax, pastel, and so on. All the drawings that appear comprise a brief exhibition of the changes that the fashion world has experienced. With this in mind, a path has been laid that starts in 1900—illustrated in watercolours—and finishes in 2000—illustrated in pencil.

My desire is to uncover the reader's desire to paint and to provide him with some of the secrets that will enable him to do so. After all, experience is the most effective way to learn, whatever the subject.

Thank you to all who have helped me to compile and improve this book

May the passion be with you.

MAITE LAFUENTE

HOW TO DRAW

The balance of a figure is the most important factor when drawing an upright pose. The image must be very straight; if this is not achieved the drawing will give the impression that the body is falling.

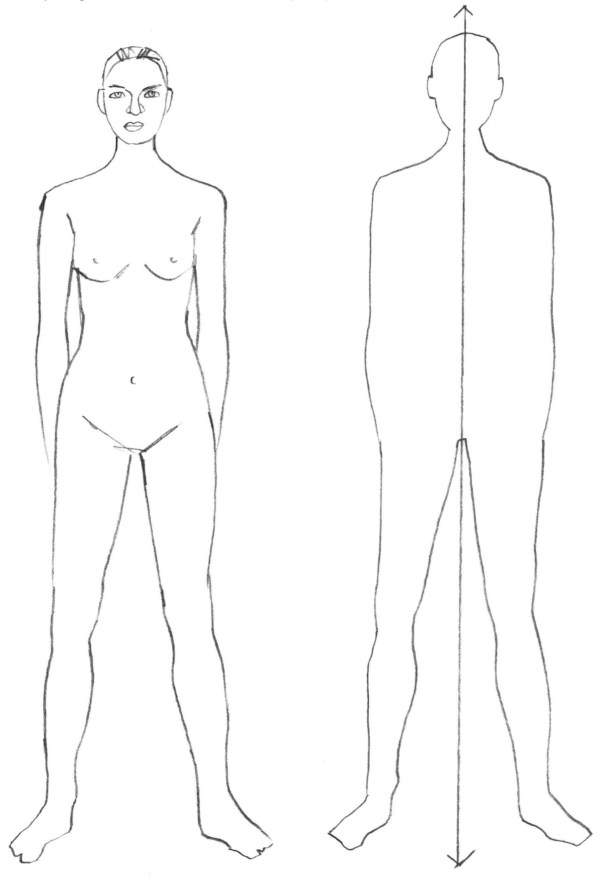

THE BODY

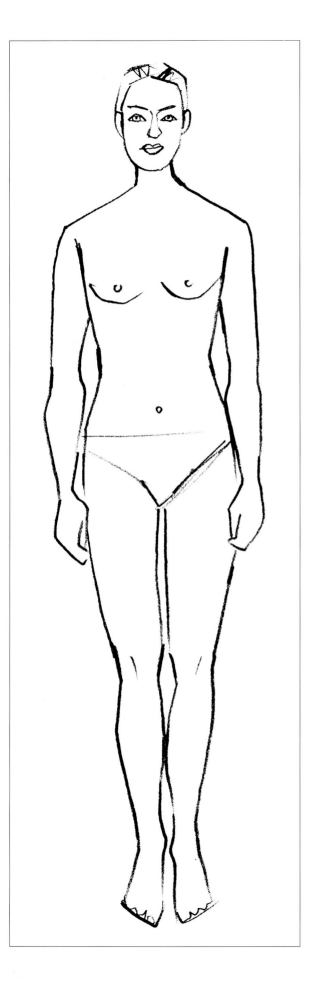

Regardless of how innovative and different the illustration may be, without some basic anatomical knowledge, it will not be precise.

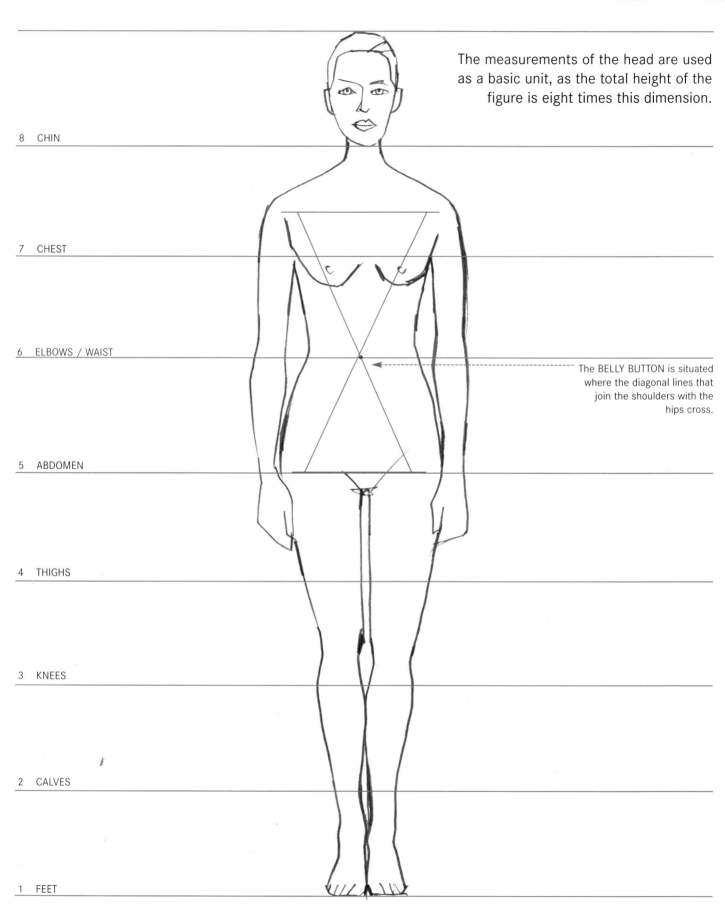

The measurements of the head are used as a basic unit, as the total height of the figure is eight times this dimension.

8   CHIN

7   CHEST

6   ELBOWS / WAIST

The BELLY BUTTON is situated where the diagonal lines that join the shoulders with the hips cross.

5   ABDOMEN

4   THIGHS

3   KNEES

2   CALVES

1   FEET

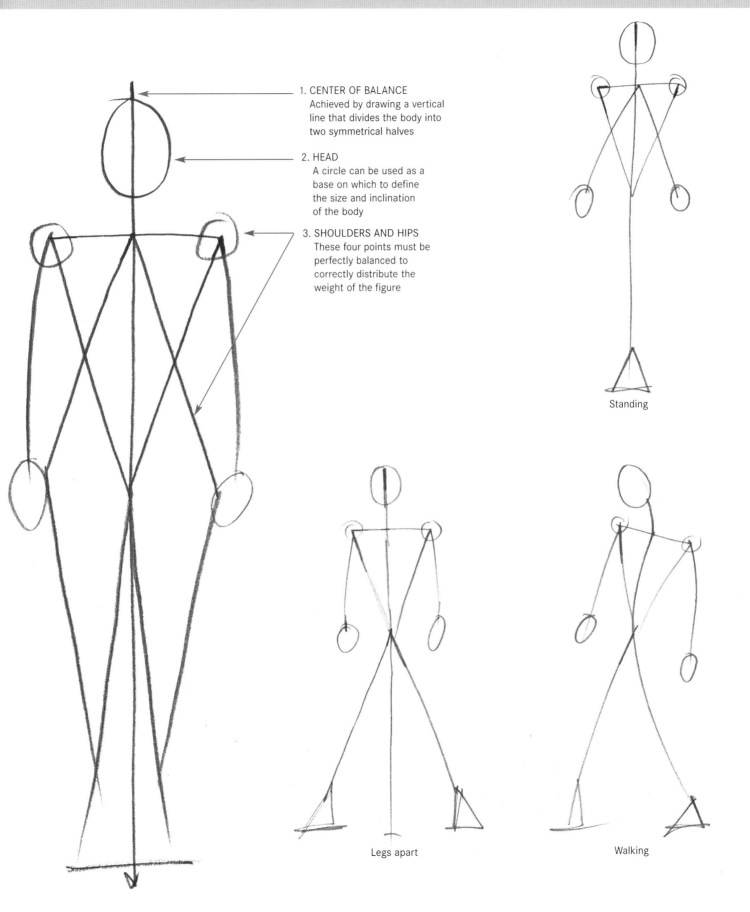

1. CENTER OF BALANCE
   Achieved by drawing a vertical
   line that divides the body into
   two symmetrical halves

2. HEAD
   A circle can be used as a
   base on which to define
   the size and inclination
   of the body

3. SHOULDERS AND HIPS
   These four points must be
   perfectly balanced to
   correctly distribute the
   weight of the figure

Standing

Legs apart

Walking

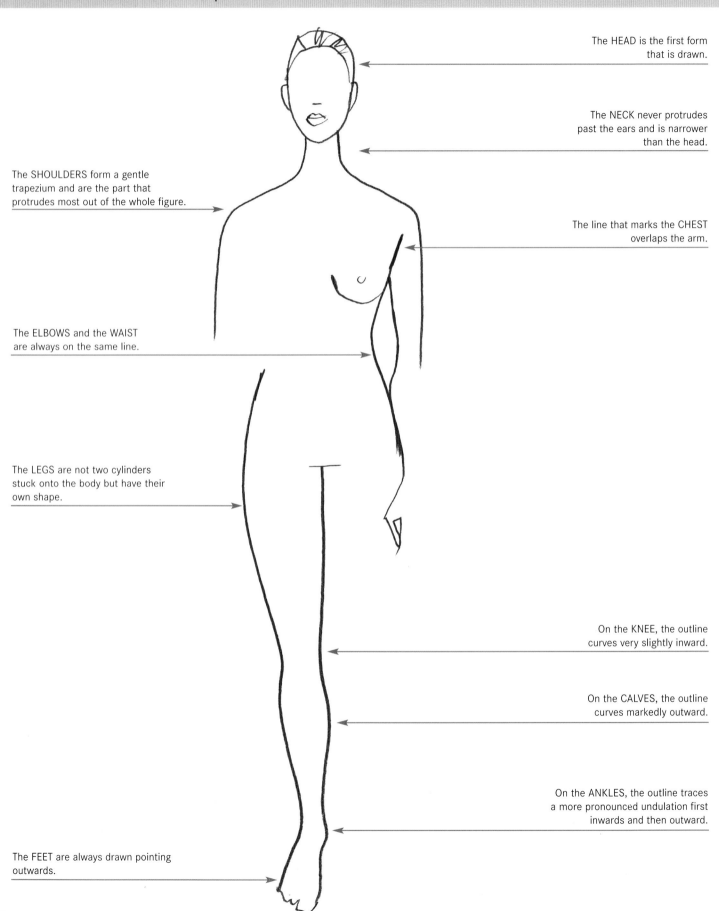

The HEAD is the first form
that is drawn.

The NECK never protrudes
past the ears and is narrower
than the head.

The SHOULDERS form a gentle
trapezium and are the part that
protrudes most out of the whole figure.

The line that marks the CHEST
overlaps the arm.

The ELBOWS and the WAIST
are always on the same line.

The LEGS are not two cylinders
stuck onto the body but have their
own shape.

On the KNEE, the outline
curves very slightly inward.

On the CALVES, the outline
curves markedly outward.

On the ANKLES, the outline traces
a more pronounced undulation first
inwards and then outward.

The FEET are always drawn pointing
outwards.

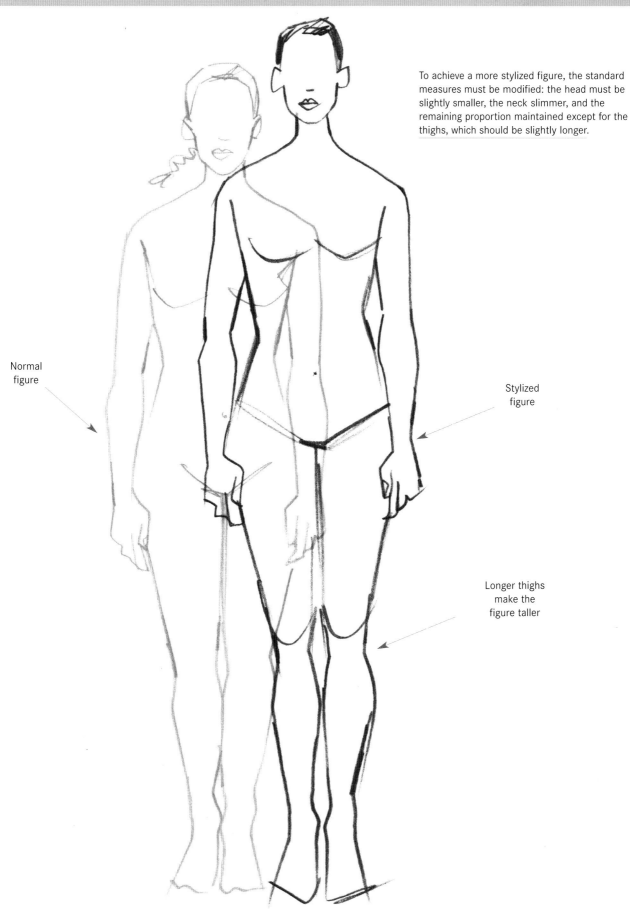

To achieve a more stylized figure, the standard measures must be modified: the head must be slightly smaller, the neck slimmer, and the remaining proportion maintained except for the thighs, which should be slightly longer.

Normal figure

Stylized figure

Longer thighs make the figure taller

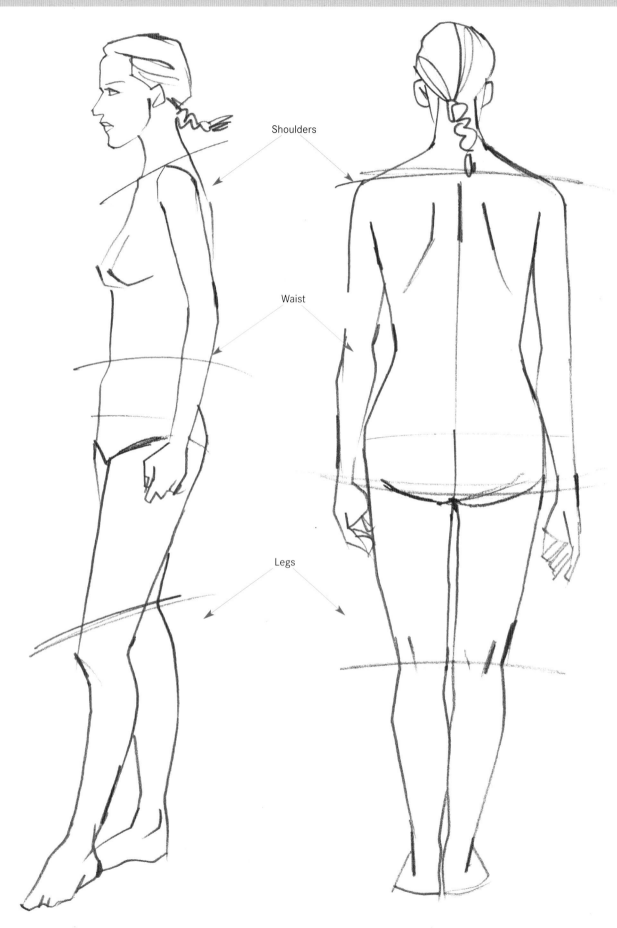

Shoulders

Waist

Legs

Situation lines

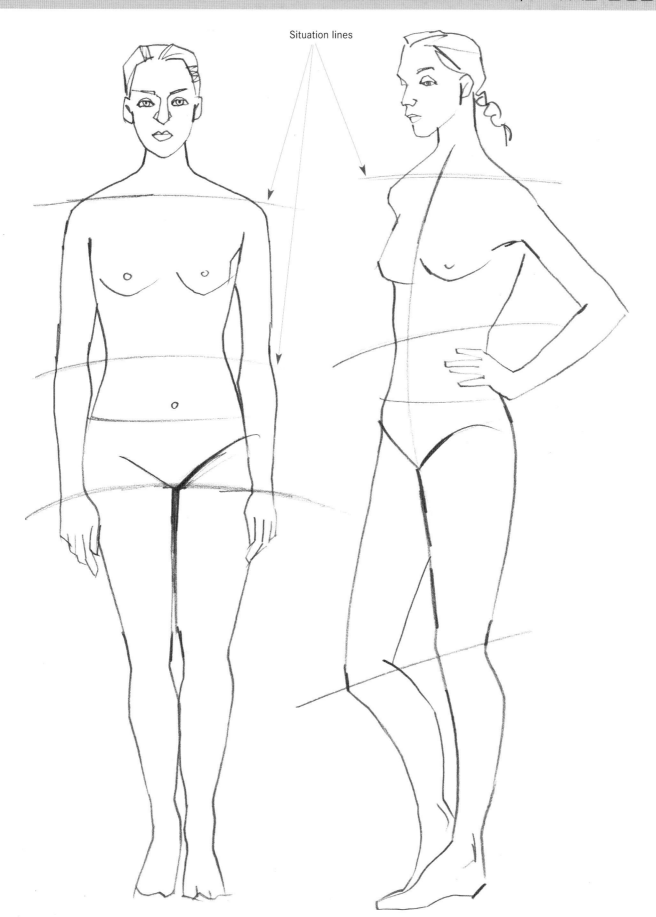

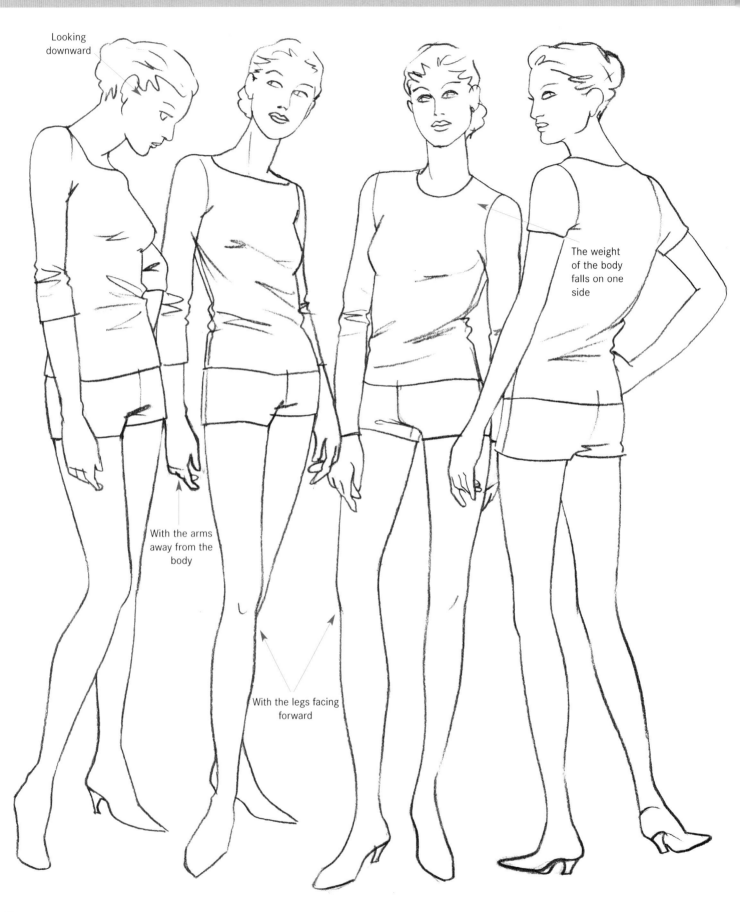

Looking downward

With the arms away from the body

With the legs facing forward

The weight of the body falls on one side

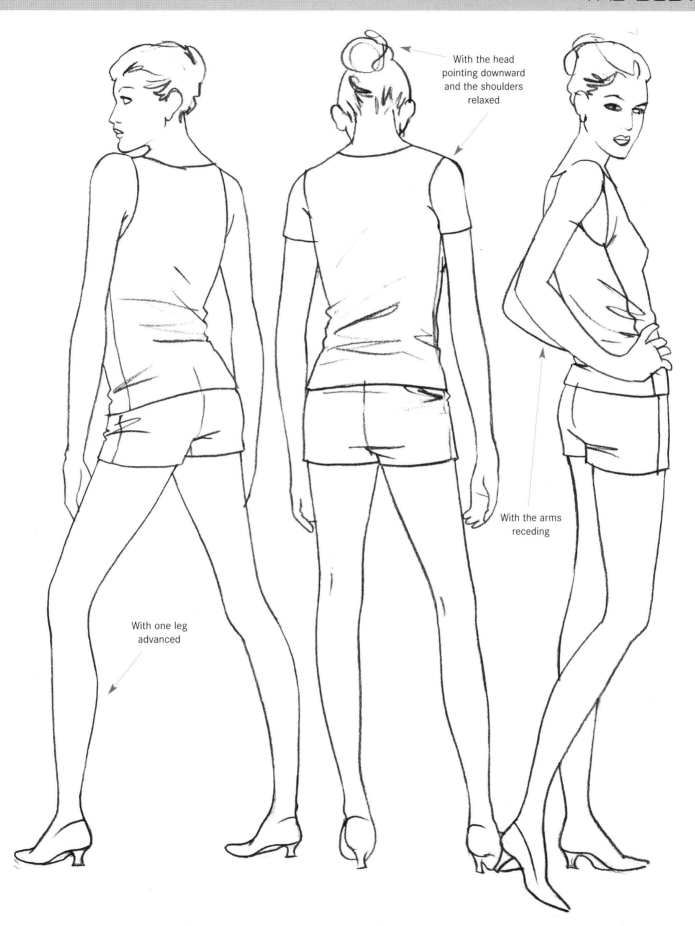

With the head
pointing downward
and the shoulders
relaxed

With the arms
receding

With one leg
advanced

In semi-profile

With the legs
apart

A shorter back leg
indicates that the
figure is tilted

When the body is tilted, the line of the trapezium is inclined to show one shoulder lower than the other

Leaning back slightly

Shoulders drooping

Feet together

Legs forwards

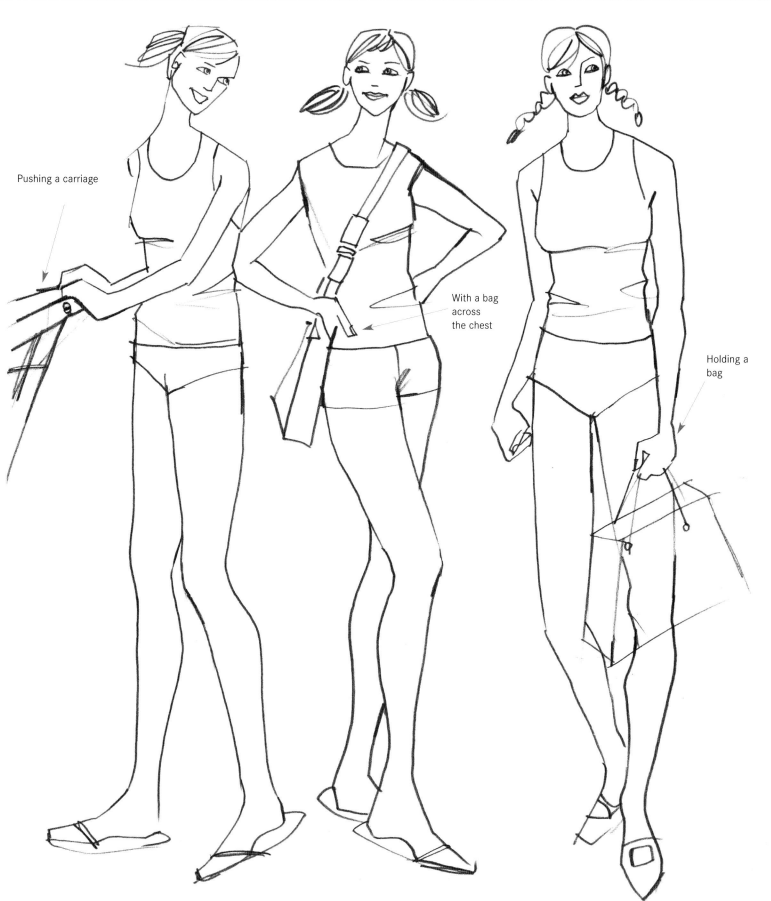

Pushing a carriage

With a bag
across
the chest

Holding a
bag

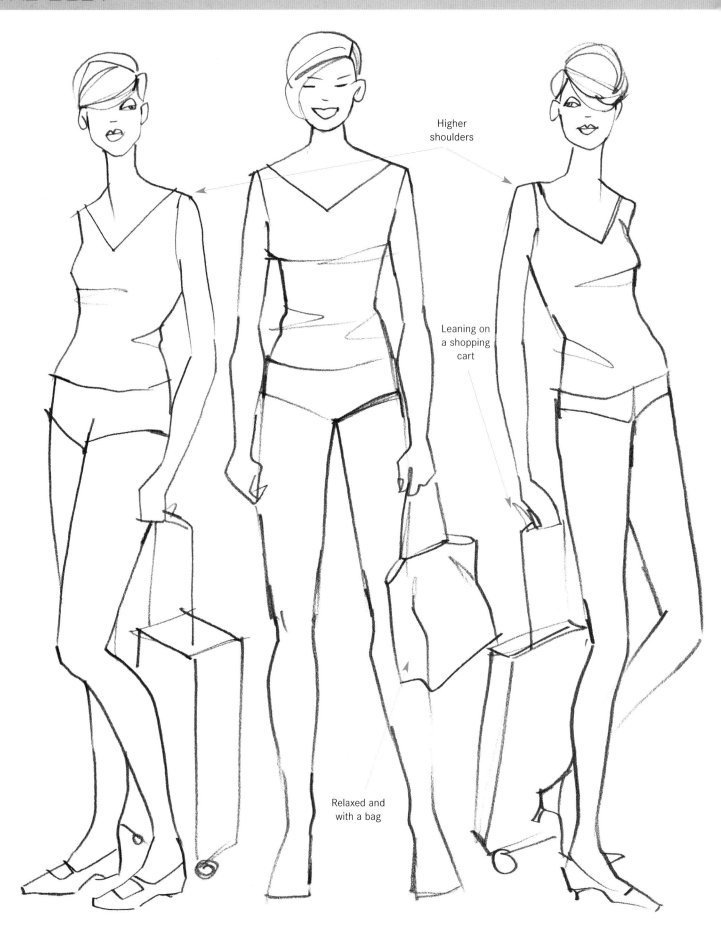

Higher
shoulders

Leaning on
a shopping
cart

Relaxed and
with a bag

Bag
receding

A hand in
the pocket
makes stronger
creases in the
trousers

When the hand is
holding something
only the thumb
is drawn

With the
arms
receding

With hand
on hip

Carrying
magazines

Arms
crossed

From behind
but looking
forward

The pronounced
inclination of the hip
makes one shoulder
lower than the other

The back leg is
only implied as
it is a complete
profile

The weight on the hands makes the body lean forward

The back leg is shorter because the body is tilted

When the arms are crossed, one hand is always hidden

Legs apart in a frontal pose

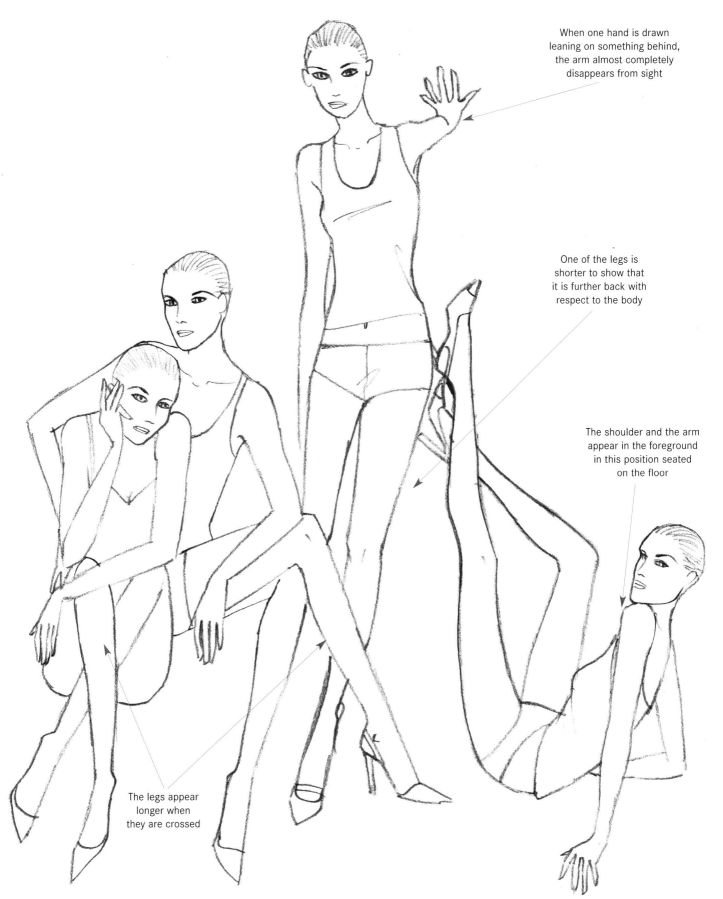

When one hand is drawn
leaning on something behind,
the arm almost completely
disappears from sight

One of the legs is
shorter to show that
it is further back with
respect to the body

The shoulder and the arm
appear in the foreground
in this position seated
on the floor

The legs appear
longer when
they are crossed

When the coat
has raglan
sleeves, the fold
is the same as
for capes

Side
stitching

The inclination of the body produces creases and folds in the clothing

The movement of the legs also produces movement in the clothes

THE HEAD AND FACE

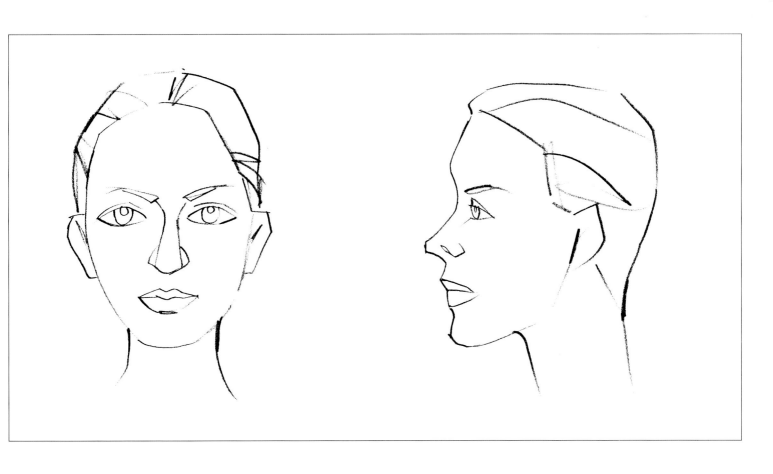

The first step in learning how to draw a face is to compile as much academic information as possible. Then, every illustrator must find his own style.

HORIZONTAL DISTRIBUTION
Horizontally, the width of the face is based on three eye lengths. That is, in the center of the face, between both eyes, there must be enough space to draw a theoretical third eye.

VERTICAL DISTRIBUTION
Vertically the face also presents three lengths of the same measurement: from the chin to the nose, the nose to the eyebrows, and the eyebrows to the hairline.

The EYEBROWS are wider next to the nose and become narrower as they approach the outer part of the face.

The EYES must be at the same level as the ears.

The upper LIP is always thinner than the lower one.

The NECK is narrower than the head and the line becomes thinner as it approaches the shoulders.

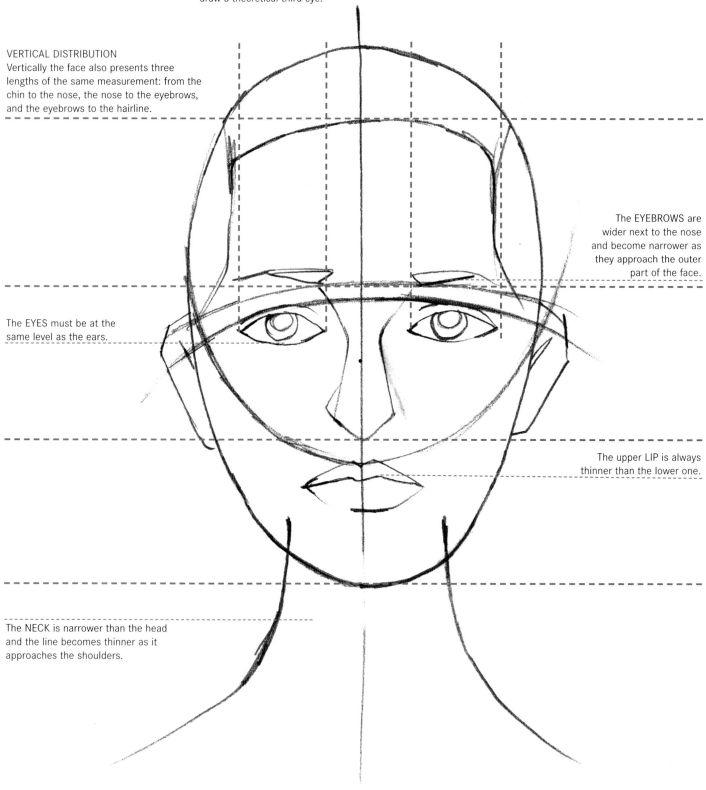

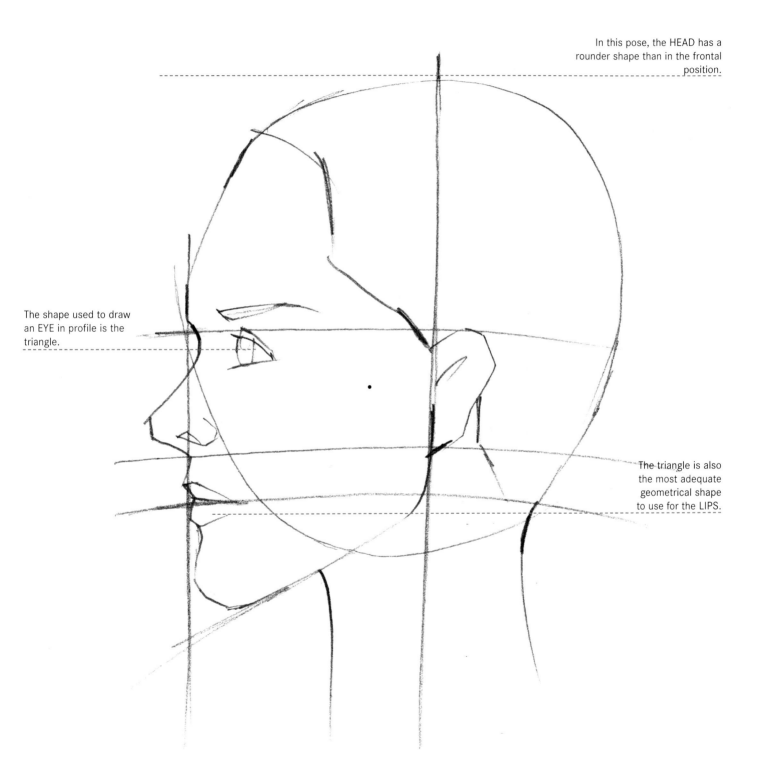

In this pose, the HEAD has a
rounder shape than in the frontal
position.

The shape used to draw
an EYE in profile is the
triangle.

The triangle is also
the most adequate
geometrical shape
to use for the LIPS.

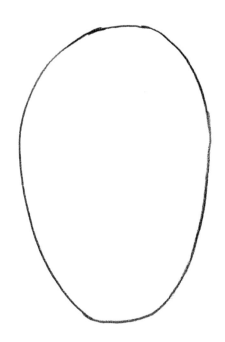

First, draw the oval

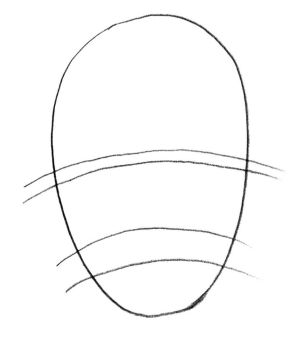

Second, mark the distribution lines

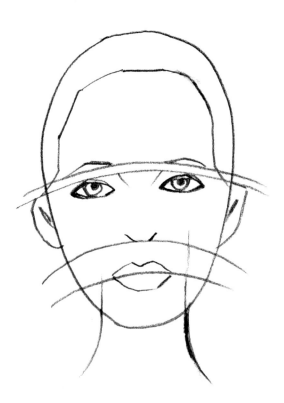

Third, draw the main parts of the face

Fourth, finish with the hair

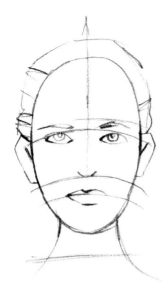

From the front

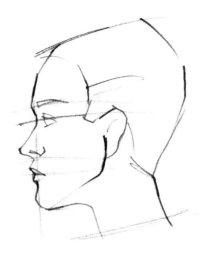

In profile

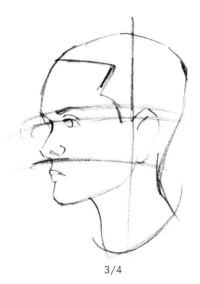

3/4

From behind

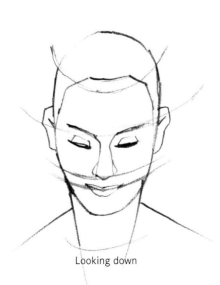

Looking down

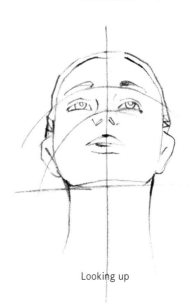

Looking up

From the front

3/4

In profile

1

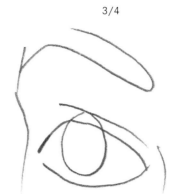

1

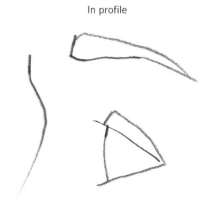

1

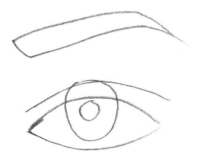

2

2

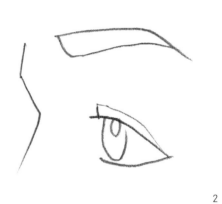

2

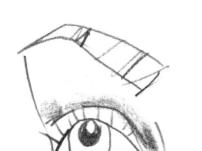

3

3

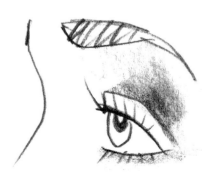

3

Exaggerated

Shaped in the style of the fifties

Heavy eyeshadow

From simple lines

In profile

From the front and closed

From the front and open

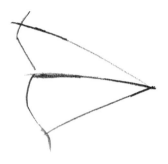

1

1

1

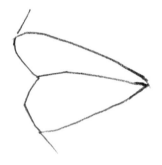

2

2

2

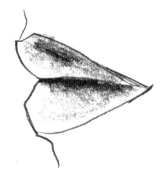

3

3

3

With simple lines

Normal

Synthesized

Draw a straight line down the side when the pose is 3/4

Ears

Nose in profile

Nose from the front

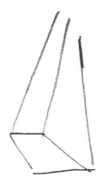

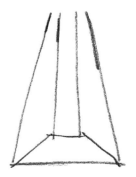

1

1

1

2

2

2

3

3

3

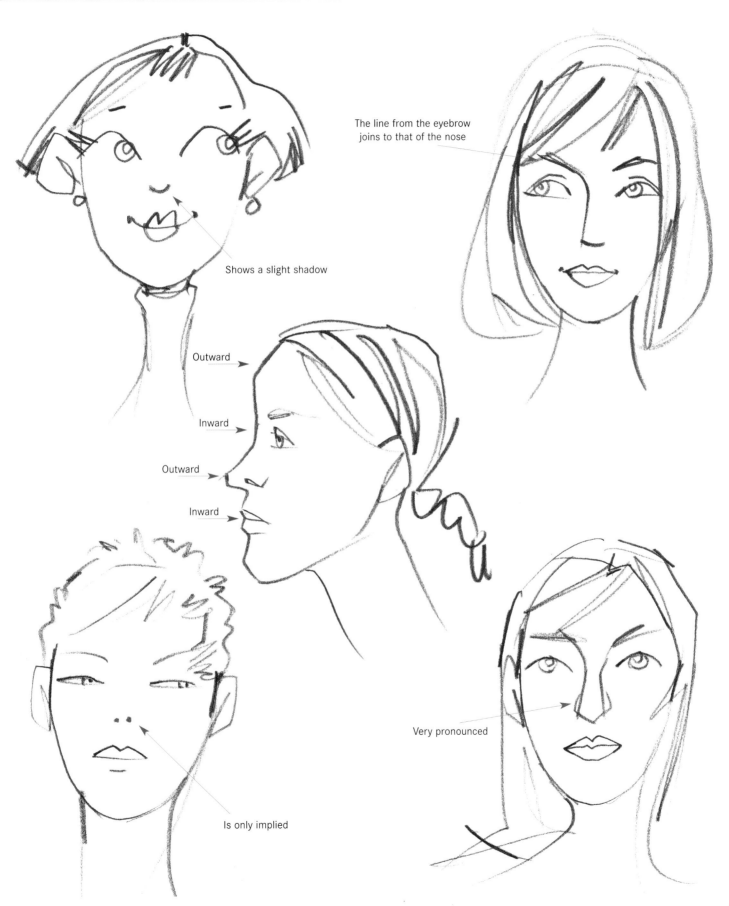

The line from the eyebrow joins to that of the nose

Shows a slight shadow

Outward

Inward

Outward

Inward

Is only implied

Very pronounced

First, choose the
hairstyle

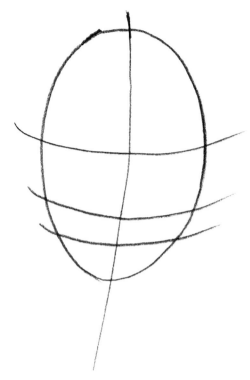

Second, draw the distribution lines

Third, mark the lines for the volume of the
hair

Fourth, finish with long lines like those made by a comb

Very pronounced and rigid hairstyles with or without a hat

Shorter hair at the nape and longer at the front part

Very high buns

With a ribbon

With fringe

With headscarf

With sun hat

Hair curly at the bottom

Masculine style hats

Hair with lots of volume

With neck scarf

Afro style hair

Hairstyle with a curl going outward

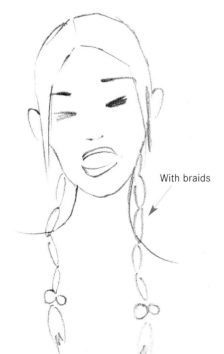

With braids

Haircut in garçon style with the fringe raised

Very glamorous hairstyles

Haircut in garçon style with the fringe to one side

Hair loose with lots of volume

ARMS AND HANDS

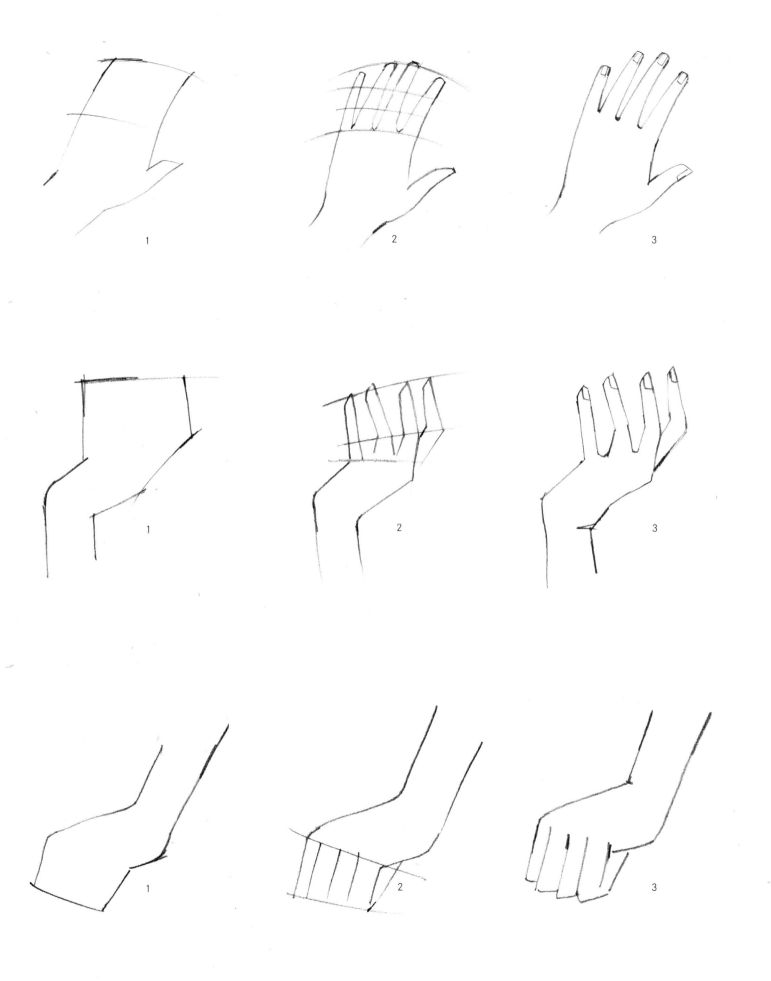

1

2

3

1

2

3

1

2

3

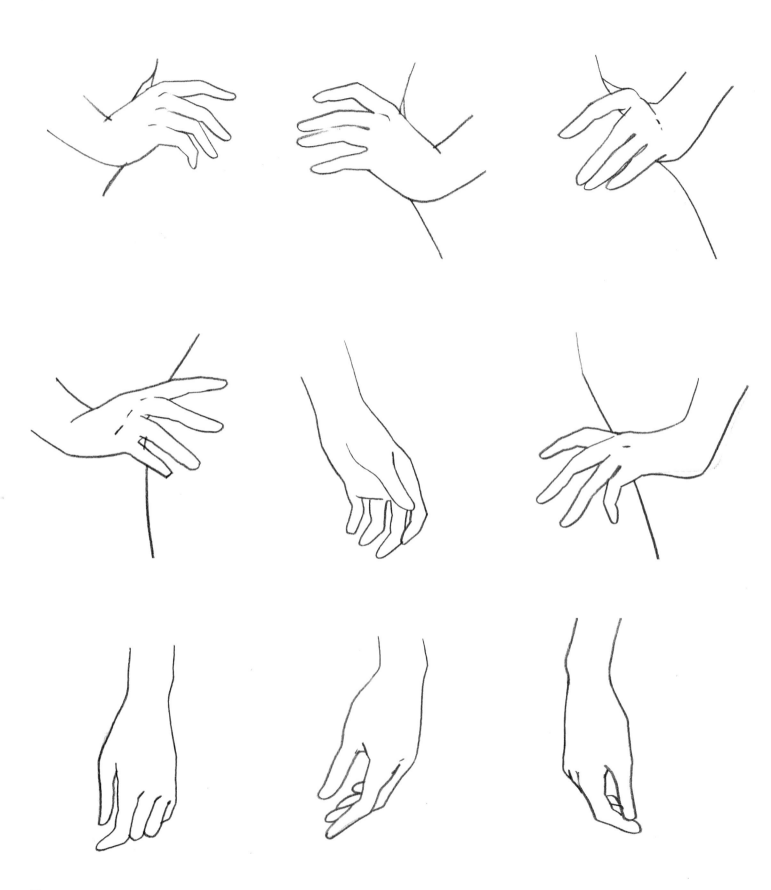

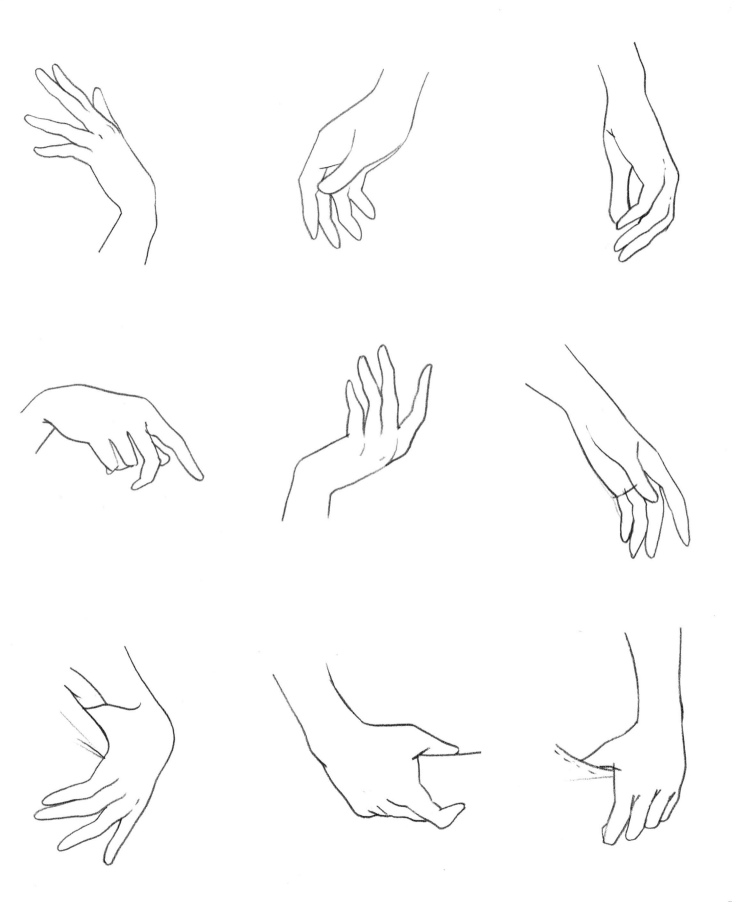

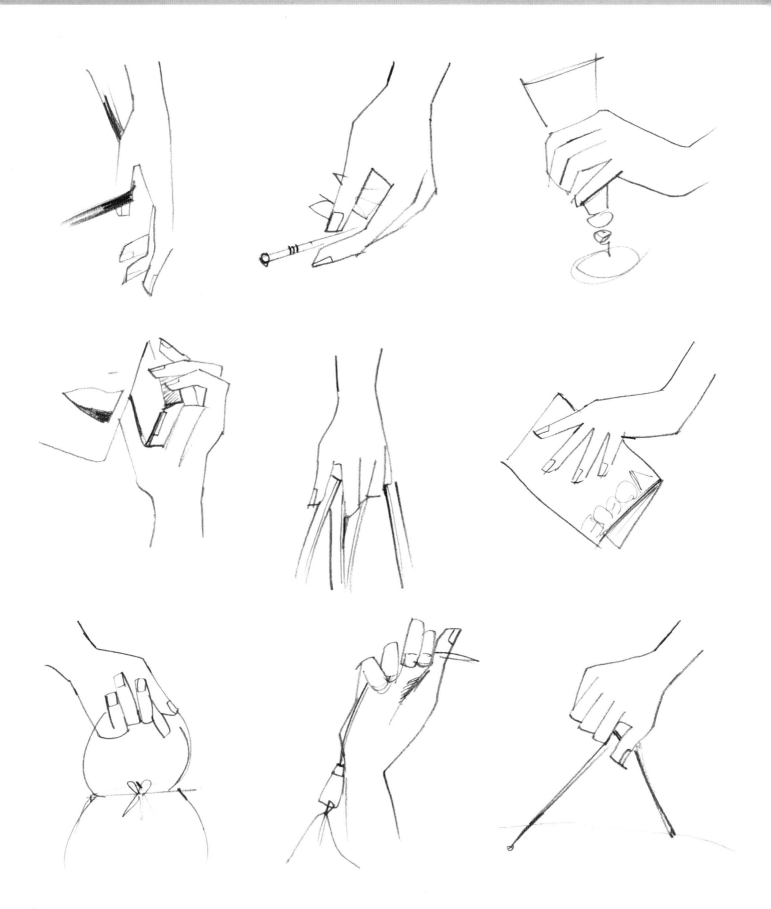

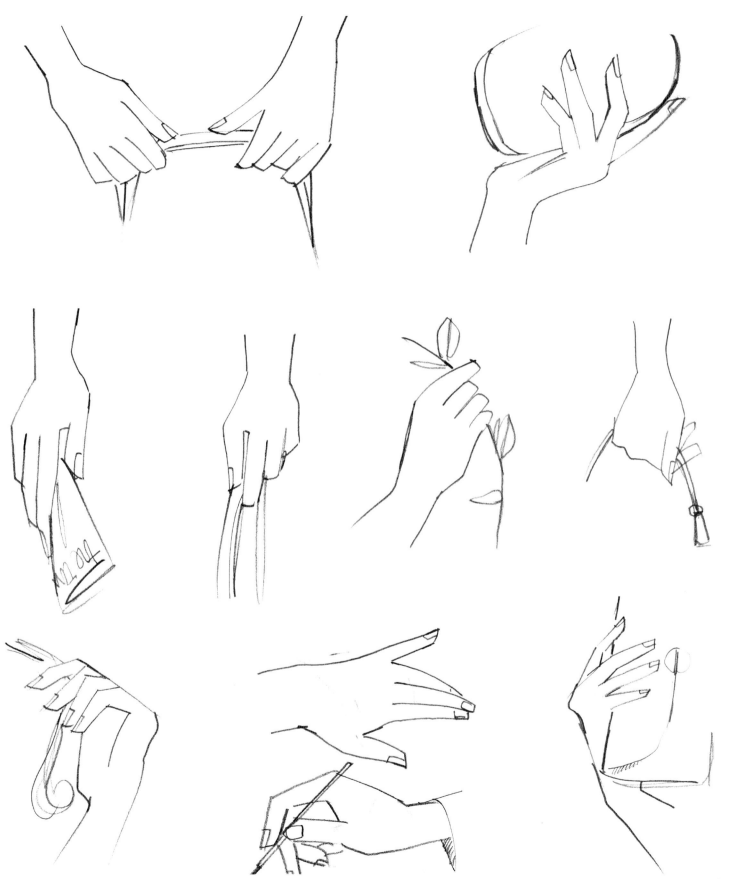

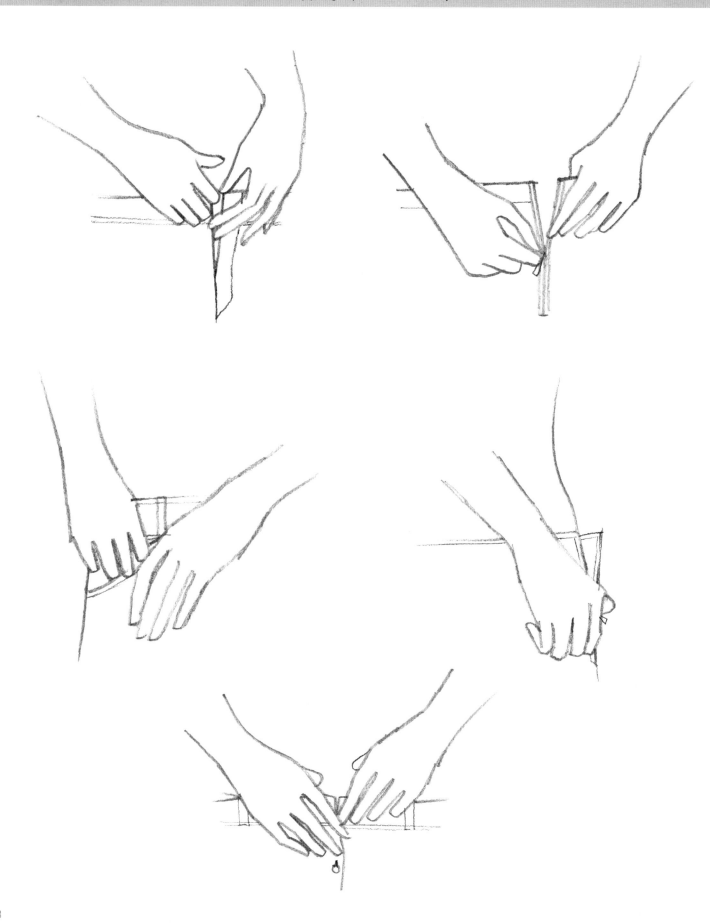

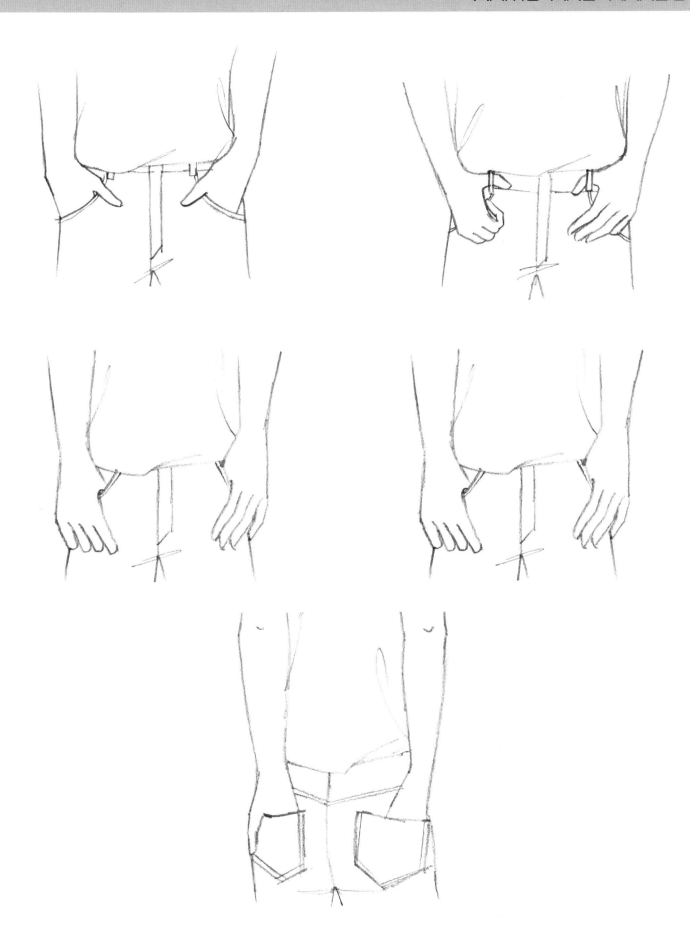

The arm resting on the abdomen creates creases in the clothing

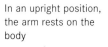

In an upright position, the arm rests on the body

When the hand rests on the hip the thumb is hidden

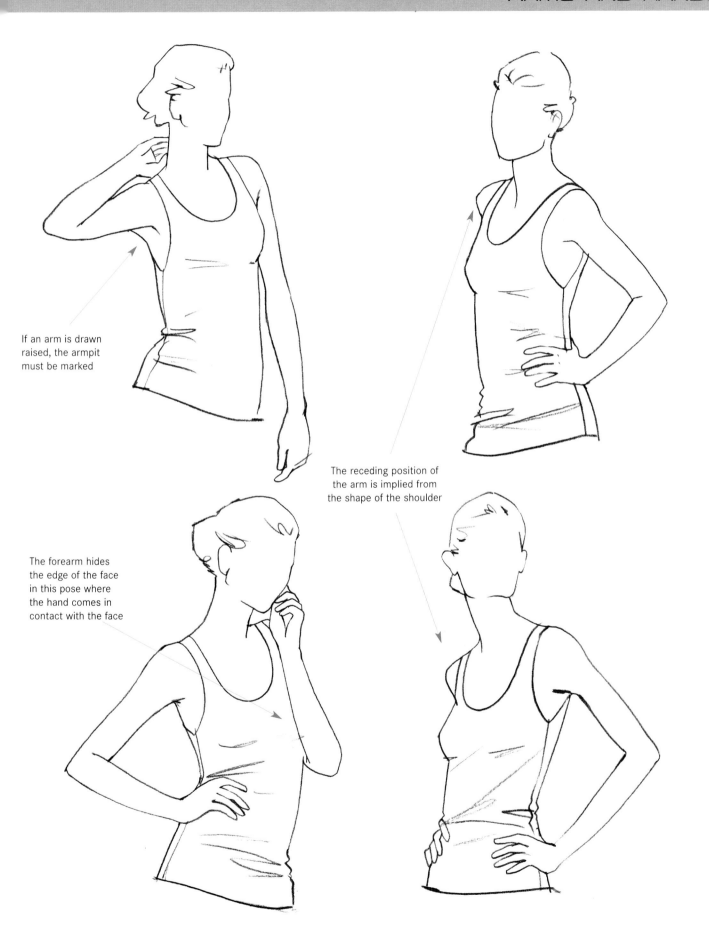

If an arm is drawn raised, the armpit must be marked

The receding position of the arm is implied from the shape of the shoulder

The forearm hides the edge of the face in this pose where the hand comes in contact with the face

When the figure has the arms
open and the elbows bent,
a zigzag line can be created
that joins the two hands

The angle of the zigzag changes depending on the pose of the figure: in the serving position with a tennis racket, the central peak almost disappears and in its place an almost straight line can be drawn.

The fingers are hidden when the hand rests on the nape just as the thumb is hidden when the hand rests on the waist.

When the hands hold objects, the thumb is normally visible

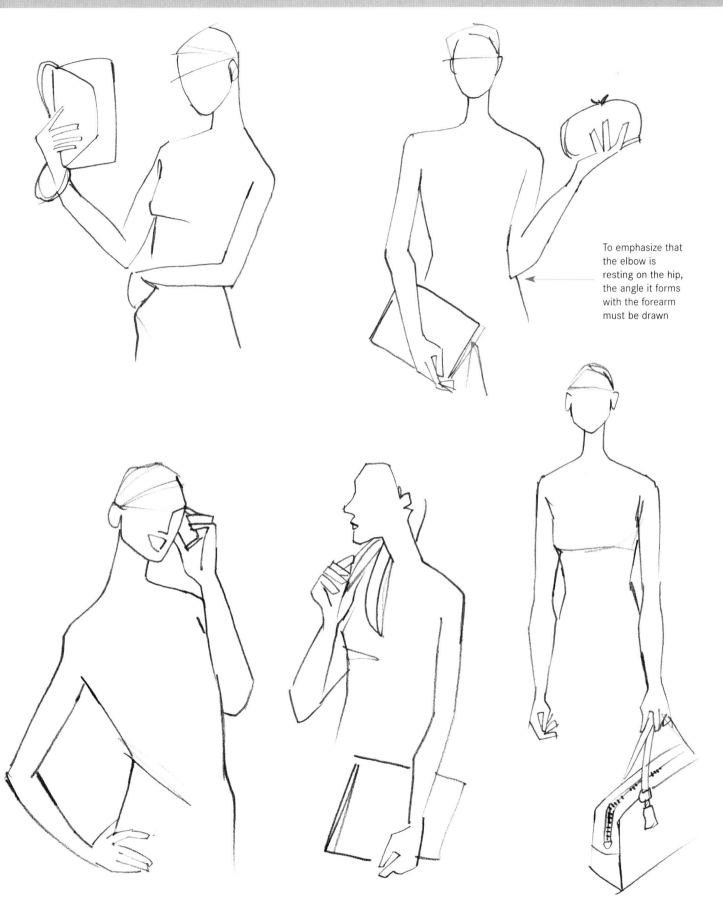

To emphasize that the elbow is resting on the hip, the angle it forms with the forearm must be drawn

LEGS AND FEET

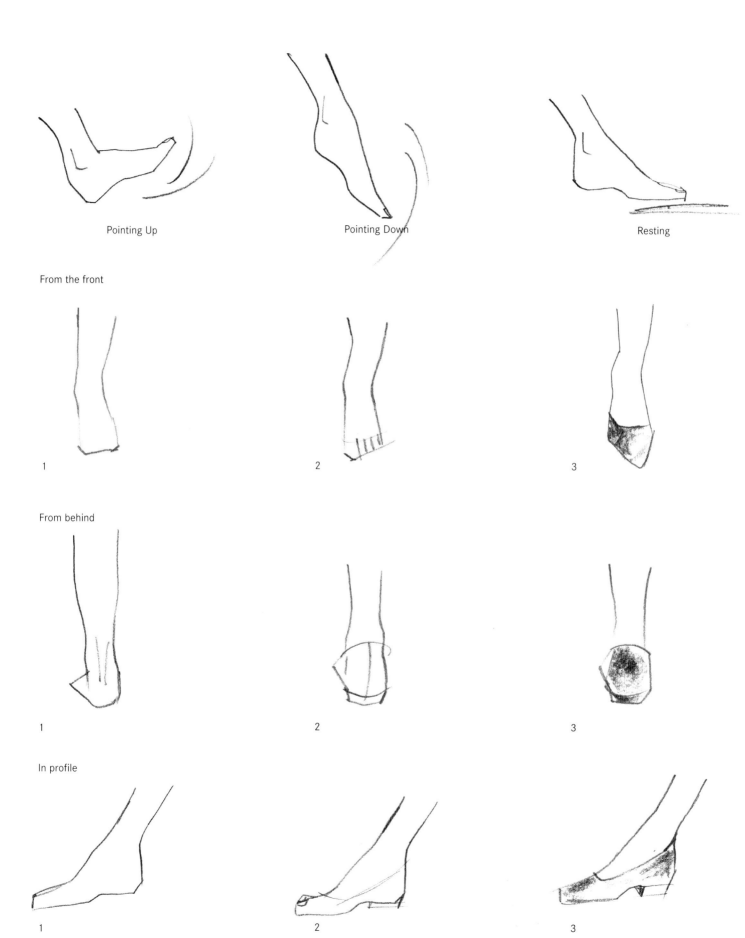

Pointing Up

Pointing Down

Resting

From the front

1

2

3

From behind

1

2

3

In profile

1

2

3

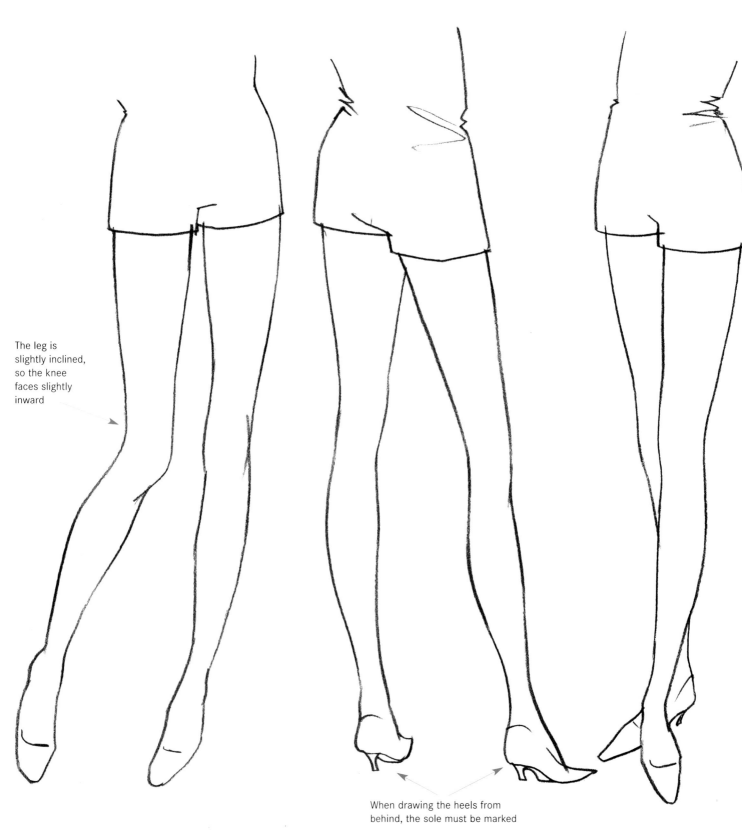

The leg is slightly inclined, so the knee faces slightly inward

When drawing the heels from behind, the sole must be marked

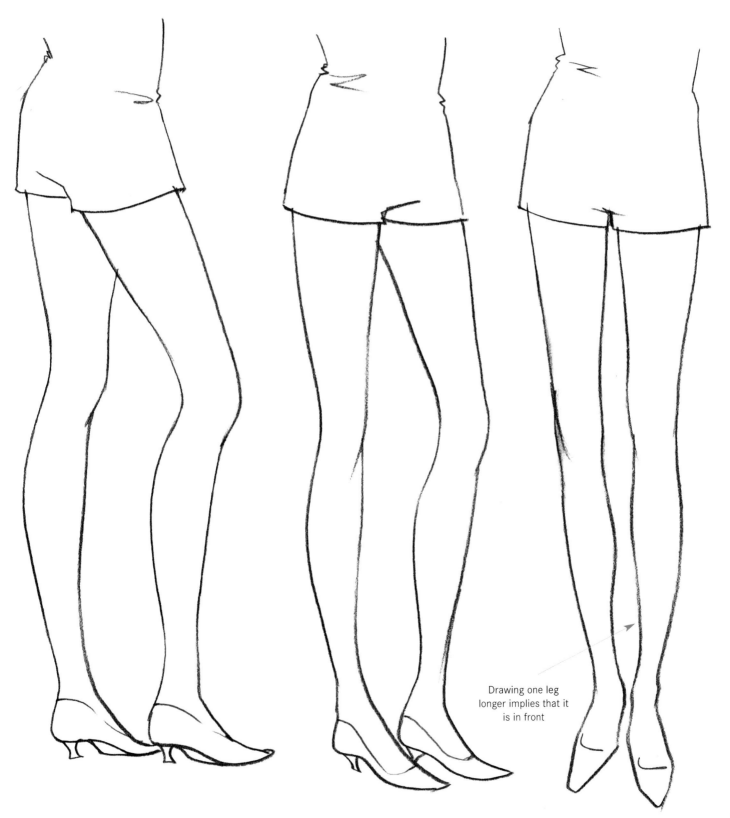

Drawing one leg
longer implies that it
is in front

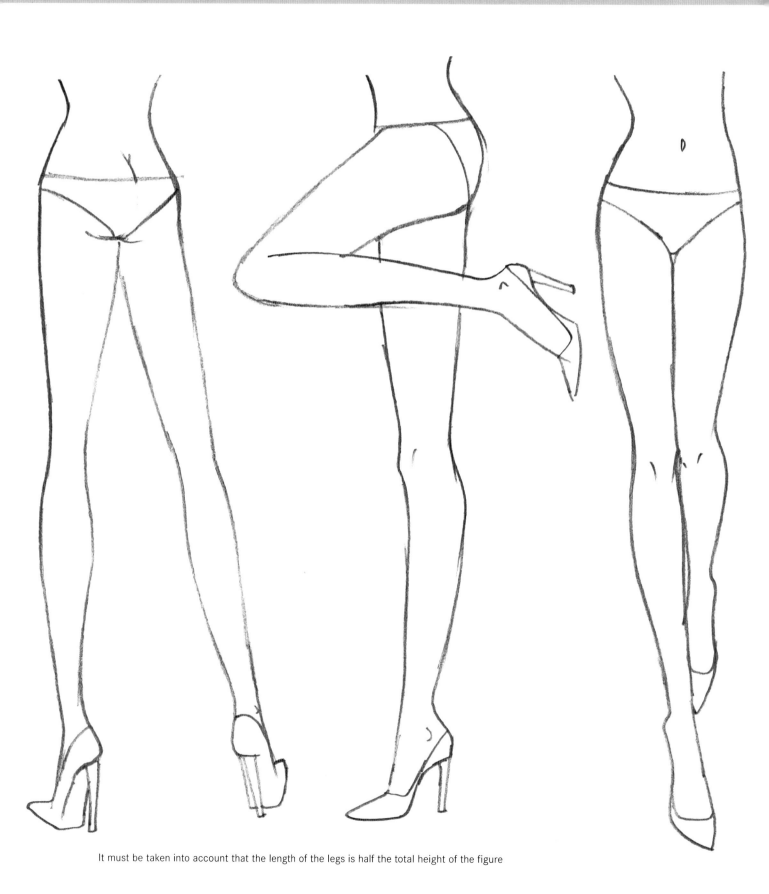

It must be taken into account that the length of the legs is half the total height of the figure

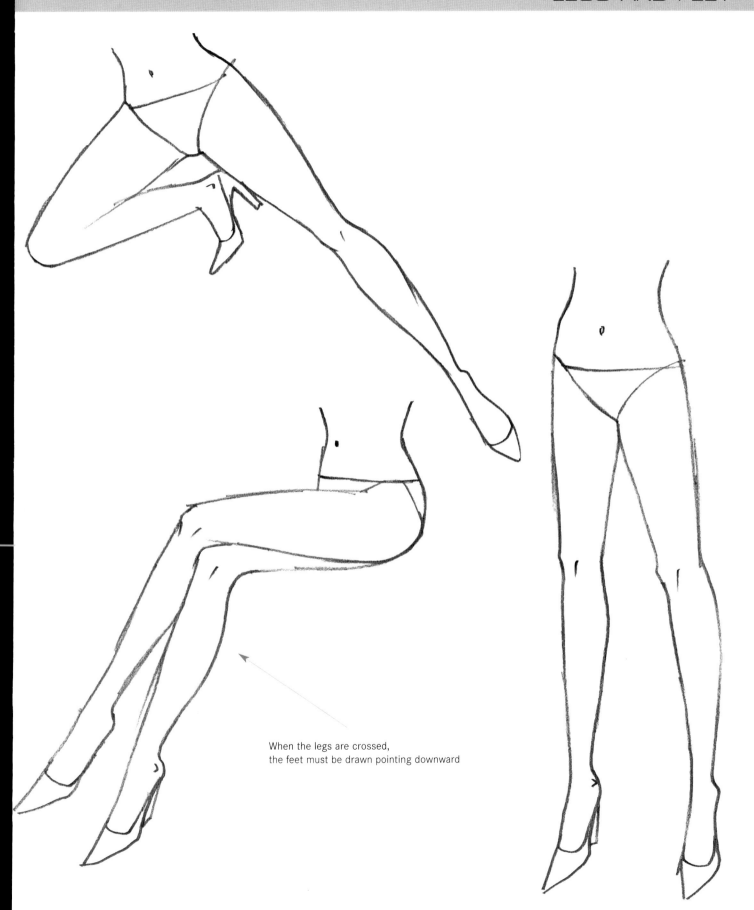

When the legs are crossed,
the feet must be drawn pointing downward

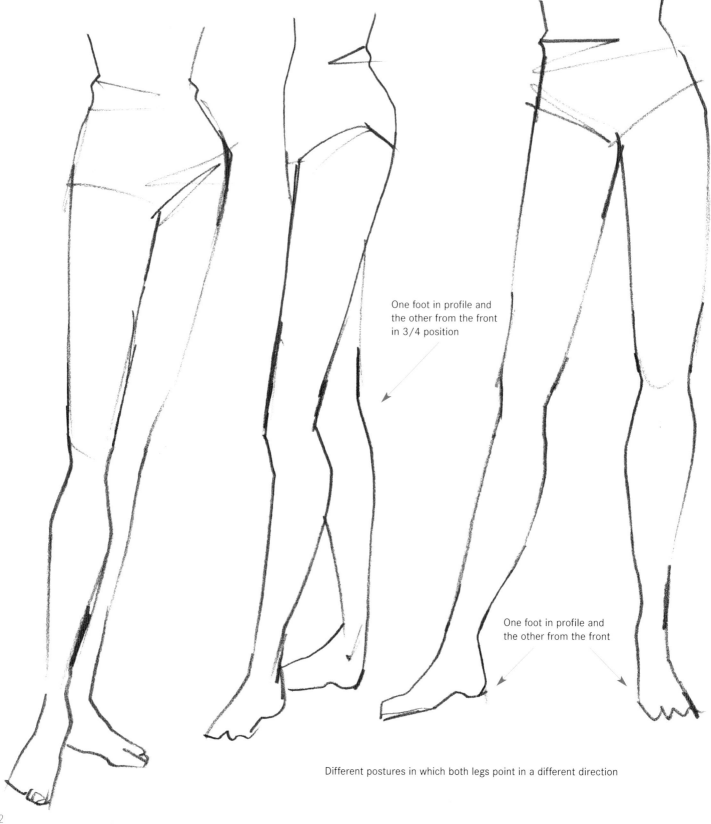

One foot in profile and
the other from the front
in 3/4 position

One foot in profile and
the other from the front

Different postures in which both legs point in a different direction

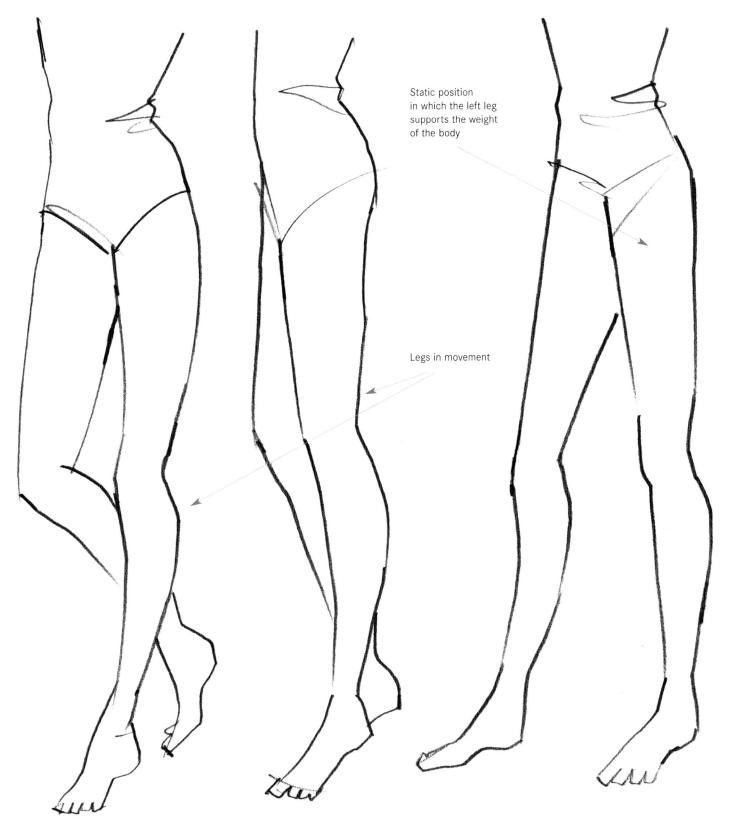

Static position
in which the left leg
supports the weight
of the body

Legs in movement

LIGHT AND SHADOW

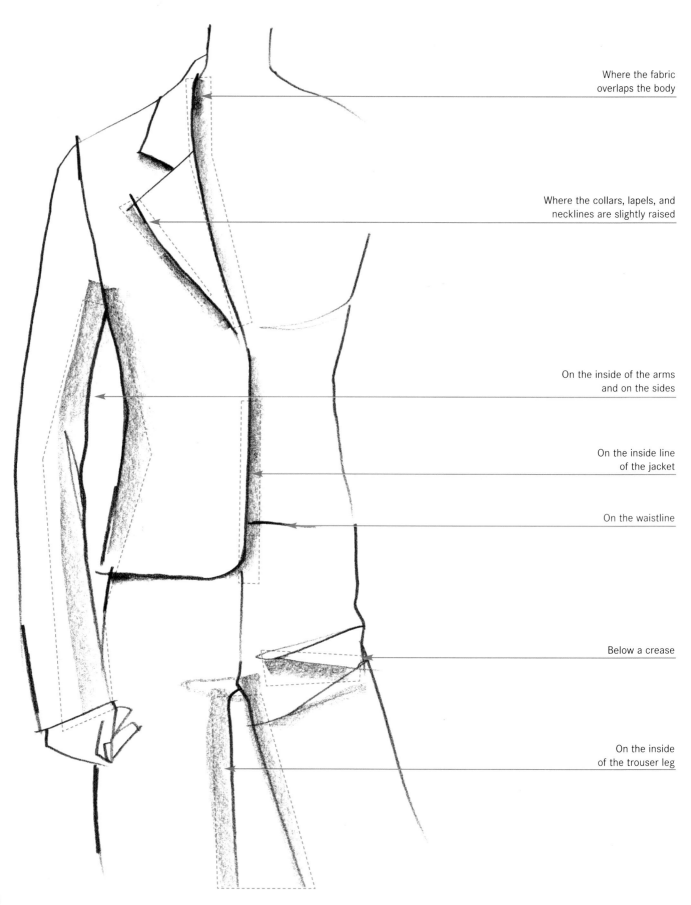

Where the fabric
overlaps the body

Where the collars, lapels, and
necklines are slightly raised

On the inside of the arms
and on the sides

On the inside line
of the jacket

On the waistline

Below a crease

On the inside
of the trouser leg

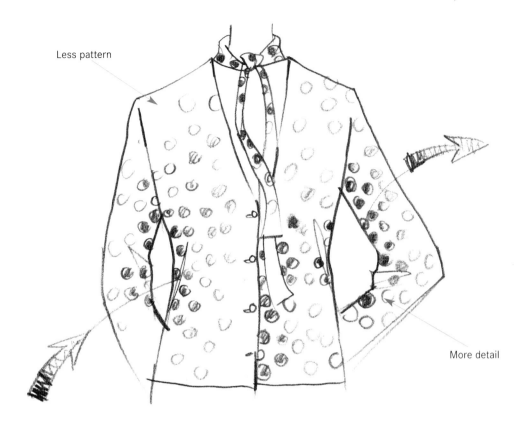

Less pattern

More detail

First, all the factors related with the light that falls upon the clothing must be studied.
Second, the drawing must start from the darker areas, for example, from the inside of the sleeve to the outside.
Third, the clothing should never be completely filled with the pattern
of the material; it should be distributed according to the intensity of the light, from greater to less.

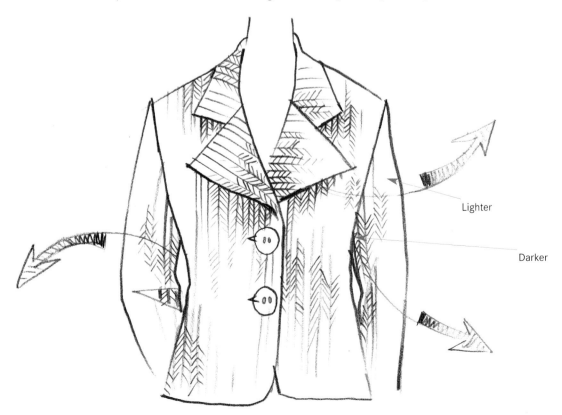

Lighter

Darker

To darken a specific area, give maximum detail to the garment's pattern (1) or shadow the area with greater intensity (2)

Draw with greater
detail as the area
receives less light

Less detail as there
is a lot of light

GARMENTS:
TECHNICAL DRAWING

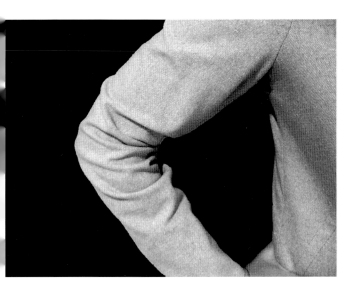

HOW TO DRAW THE FALL OF FABRIC

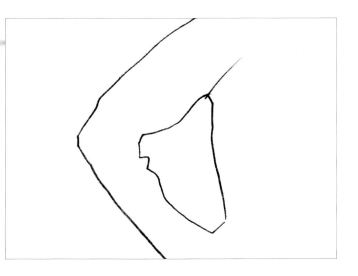

1st Draw the outline

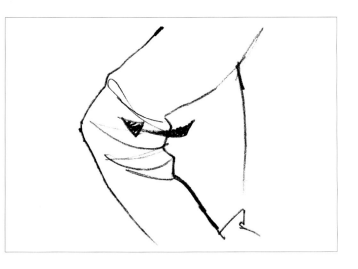

2nd Squint your eyes and draw only the most visible creases. SYNTHESIZE!

3rd Draw the creases away from the gesture, never the other way round.

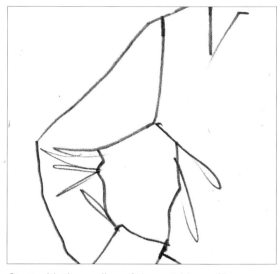

Start with the outline of the outside profile

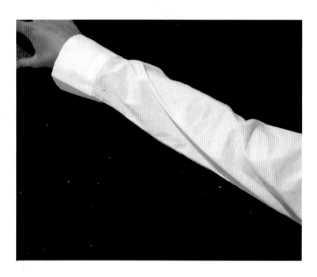

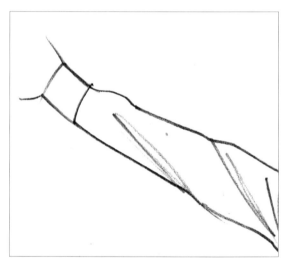

Half-close your eyes and draw
only the creases that stand out most

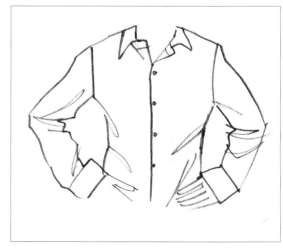

Draw the line of the crease starting from where
the movement goes outward and never vice versa

 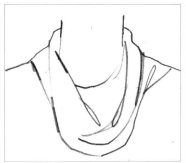  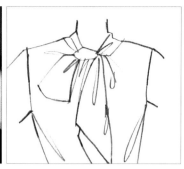

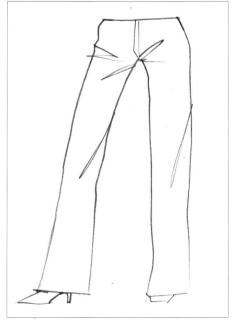  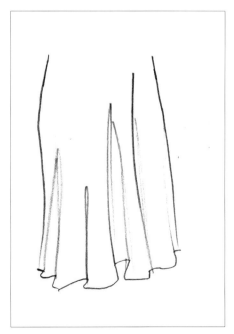

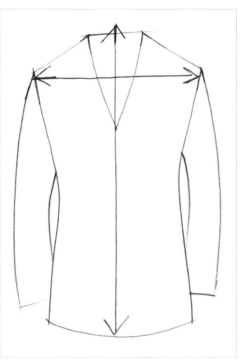

First establish the axels of symmetry

The curves and folds lend realism to the drawing

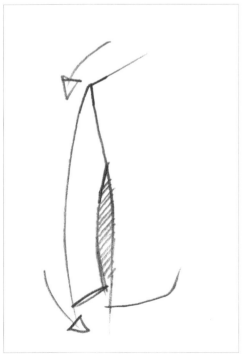

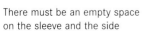
There must be an empty space
on the sleeve and the side

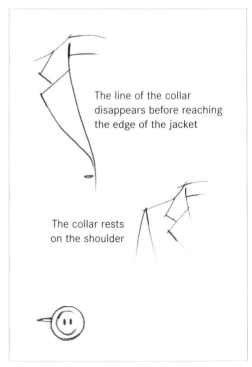

The line of the collar
disappears before reaching
the edge of the jacket

The collar rests
on the shoulder

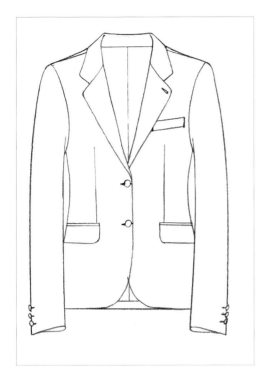

Tailored jacket

Blazer

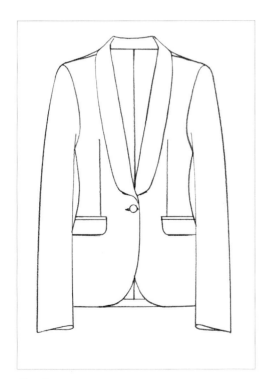

Tuxedo

Retro style

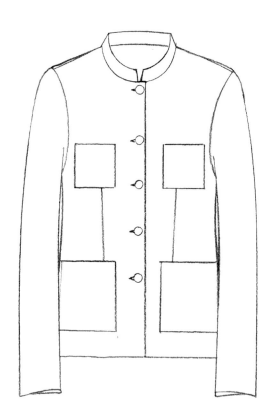

Mao

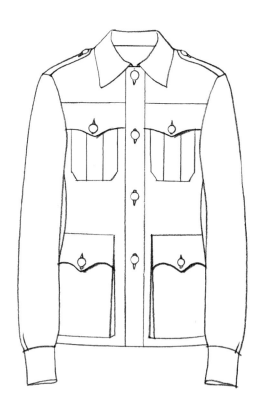

Saharan

Navy

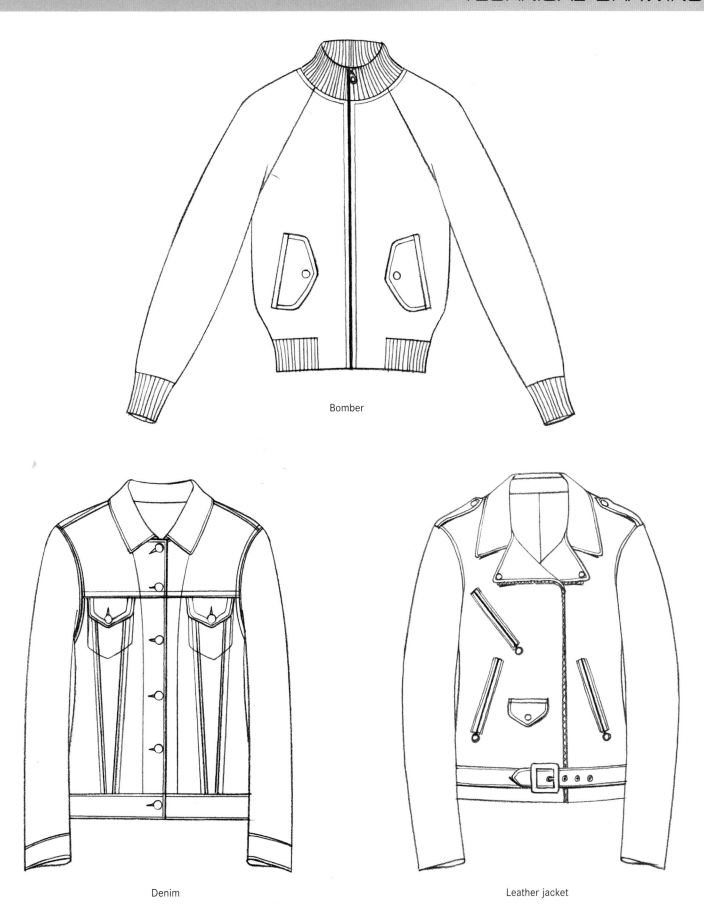

Bomber

Denim

Leather jacket

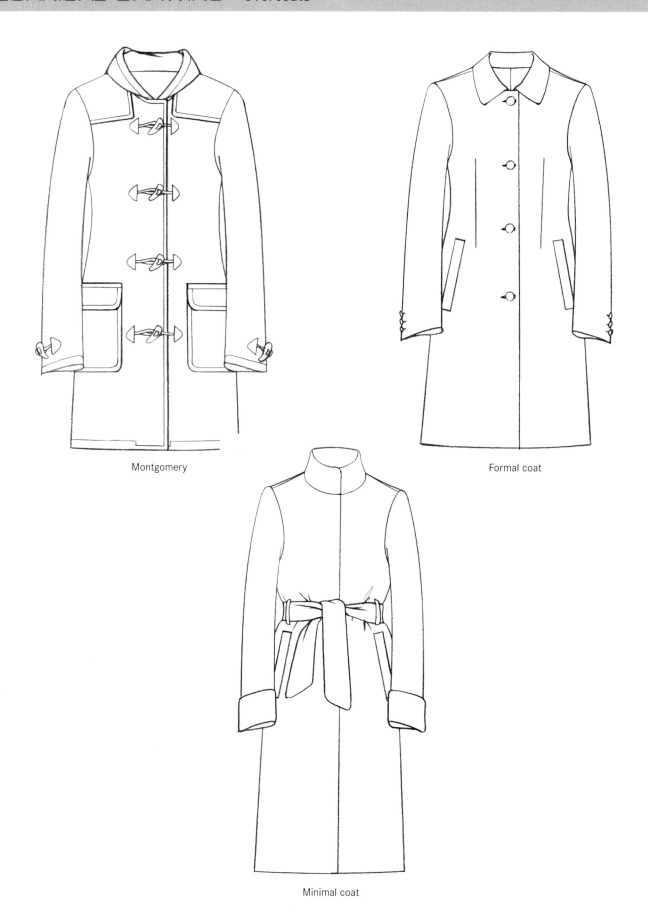

Montgomery

Formal coat

Minimal coat

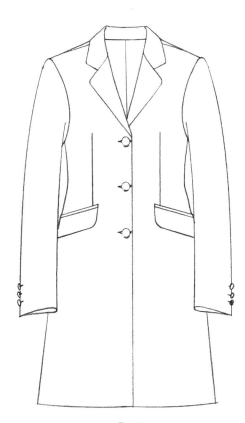

Frock coat

Double-breasted coat

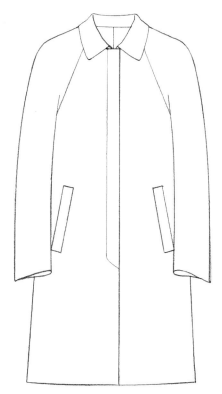

Raincoat

Cape

Jeans

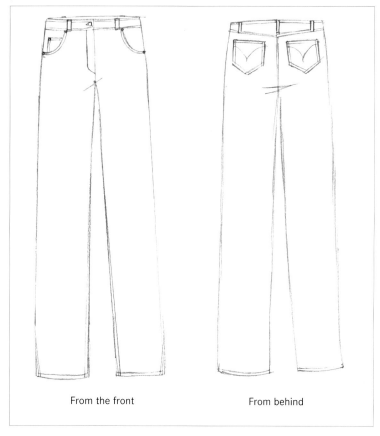

From the front

From behind

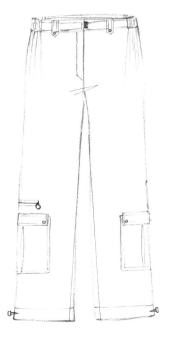

Cargo 3/4

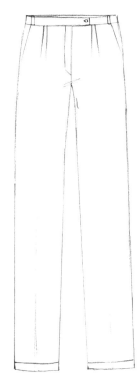

Tailored trousers

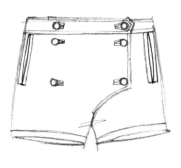

Navy shorts

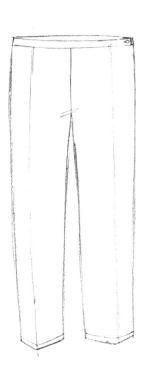

Pirate

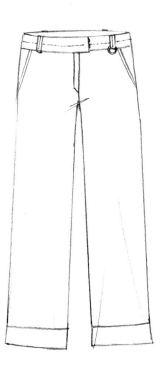

Fishing

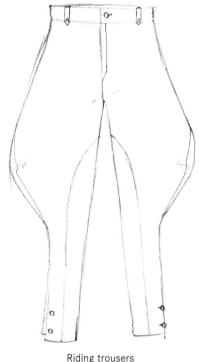

Riding trousers

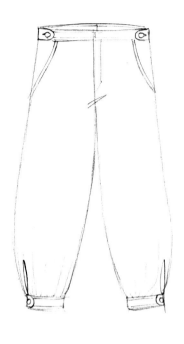

Plus-fours

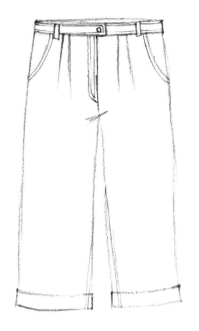

Bermuda shorts

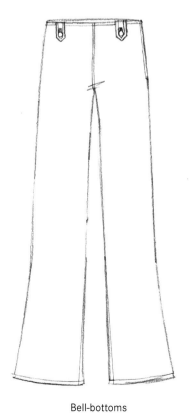

Bell-bottoms

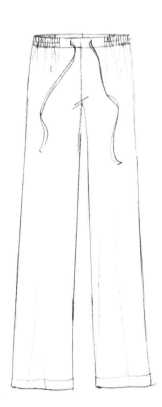

Pajamas

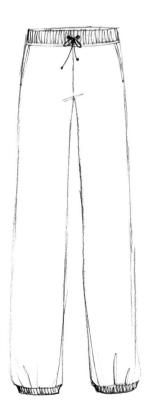

Tracksuit trousers

Pleated

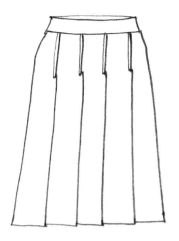

With folds

Crossed miniskirt

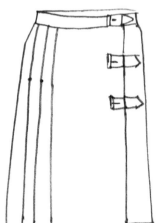

Gusset-fold skirt

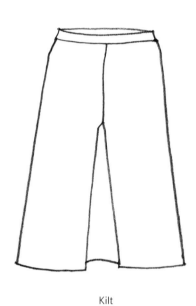

Kilt

Trouser skirt

Sarong

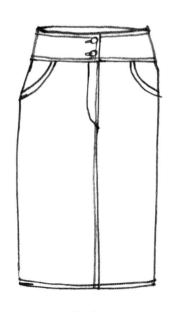

Denim

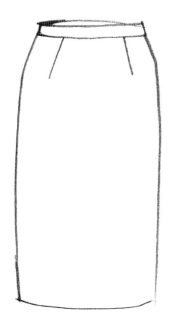

Tailored skirt

Cape

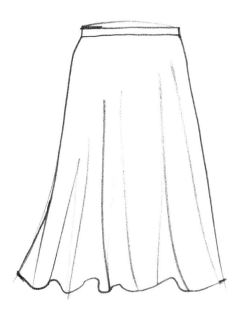

Bias

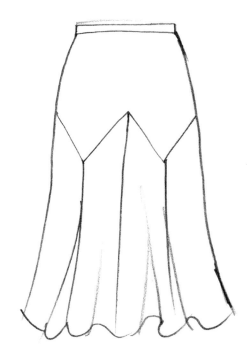

With godets

With frills

Balloon

Basic

Denim shirt

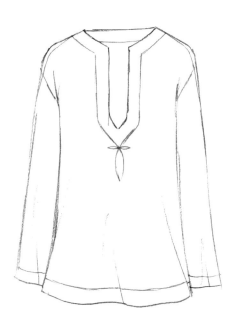

Kaftan

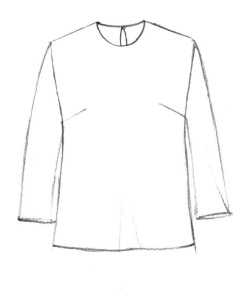

With 3/4 length sleeves

Basic

Smock

Cache-coeur

Thirties, feminine shirt collar

Fifties, tied

Chinese buttoned

Shirt dress

Little black dress

Halter or Marylin

Twenties, cut to the hips

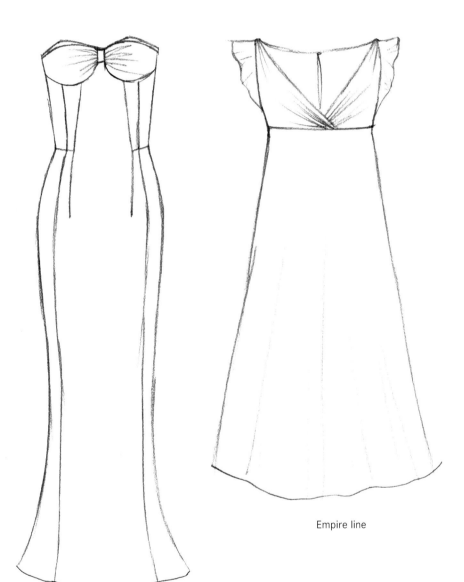

Mermaid

Empire line

Fifties, off the shoulder

Flat knitting machine

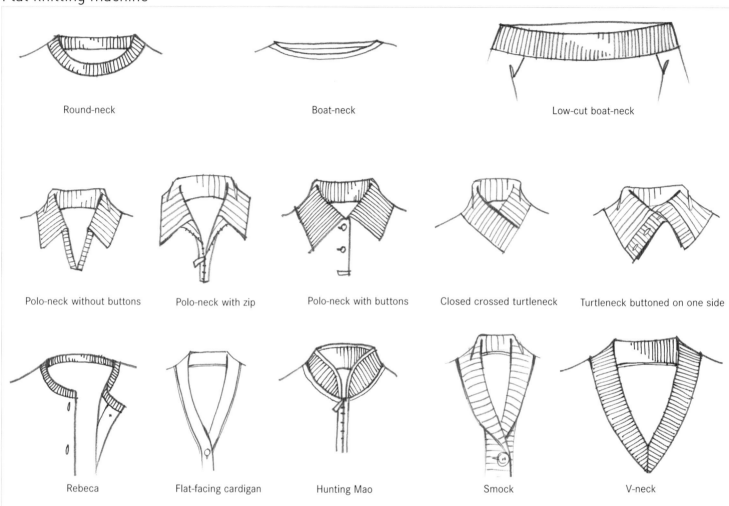

Round-neck

Boat-neck

Low-cut boat-neck

Polo-neck without buttons

Polo-neck with zip

Polo-neck with buttons

Closed crossed turtleneck

Turtleneck buttoned on one side

Rebeca

Flat-facing cardigan

Hunting Mao

Smock

V-neck

Circular knitting machine

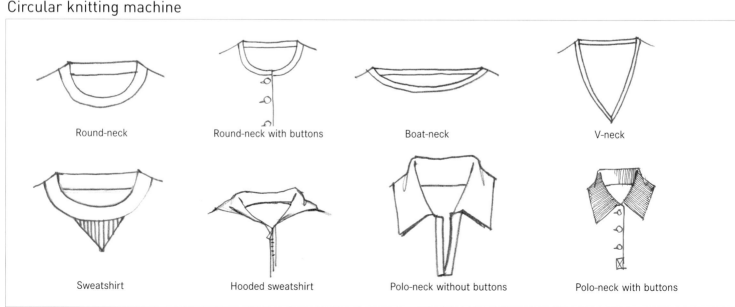

Round-neck

Round-neck with buttons

Boat-neck

V-neck

Sweatshirt

Hooded sweatshirt

Polo-neck without buttons

Polo-neck with buttons

Tricotosa

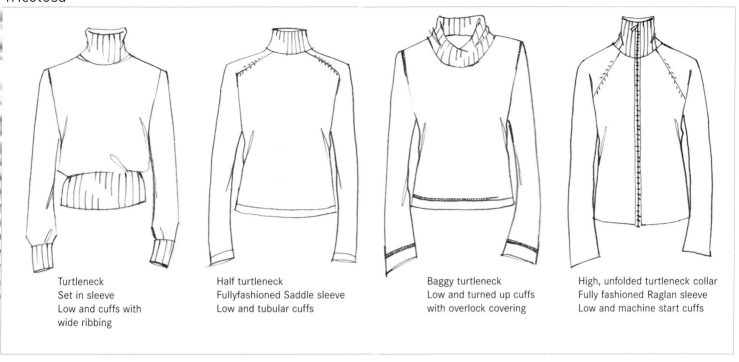

Turtleneck
Set in sleeve
Low and cuffs with
wide ribbing

Half turtleneck
Fullyfashioned Saddle sleeve
Low and tubular cuffs

Baggy turtleneck
Low and turned up cuffs
with overlock covering

High, unfolded turtleneck collar
Fully fashioned Raglan sleeve
Low and machine start cuffs

Circular knitting machine

Marcel

Cache-coeur

Low-cut word of honor

Ruffled
turtleneck collar

Low-cut boat-neck and 3/4 length sleeves

Jogging bottoms

Fusseau trousers

Wide trousers

The patterns and reliefs of knitted clothing – such as cable, Aran, openwork, jacquard, intarsia – must be drawn following a gradient of greater to less definition, following the intensity of the light and always starting with the darker areas. The garment should never be filled in completely.

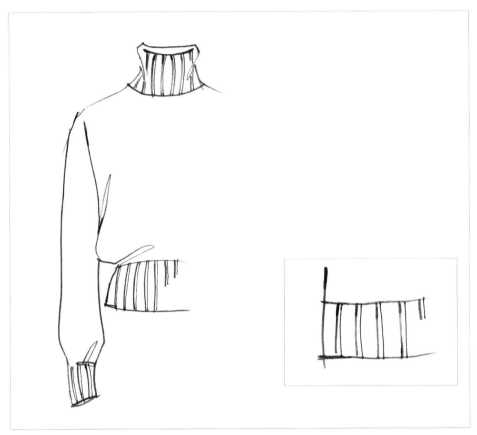

Thick stitch ribbing

It is very important to know how to differentiate a thick ribbing from a thin one. To do this, put the stripes more or less together. It is also necessary to differentiate the stitches that go backward from those that go forward and to leave the spaces more closed or open depending on the ribbing.

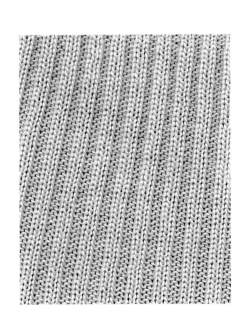

Thin stitch ribbing

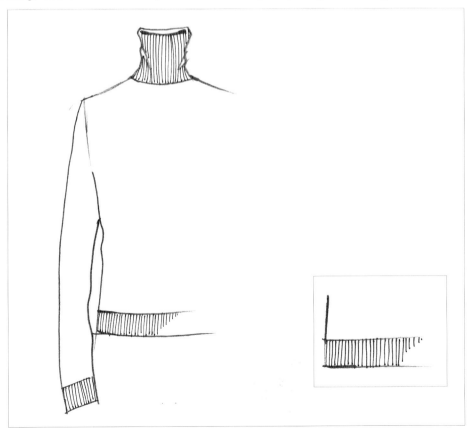

ACCESSORIES

Hats
Sun hats
Berets
Headscarves

Mule

Ballroom

It is important to draw the
bottom of the heel to reflect
the perspective

Sixties high heels

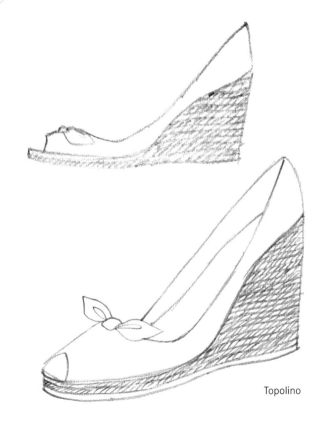

Topolino

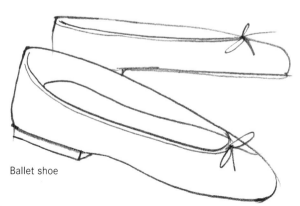

Ballet shoe

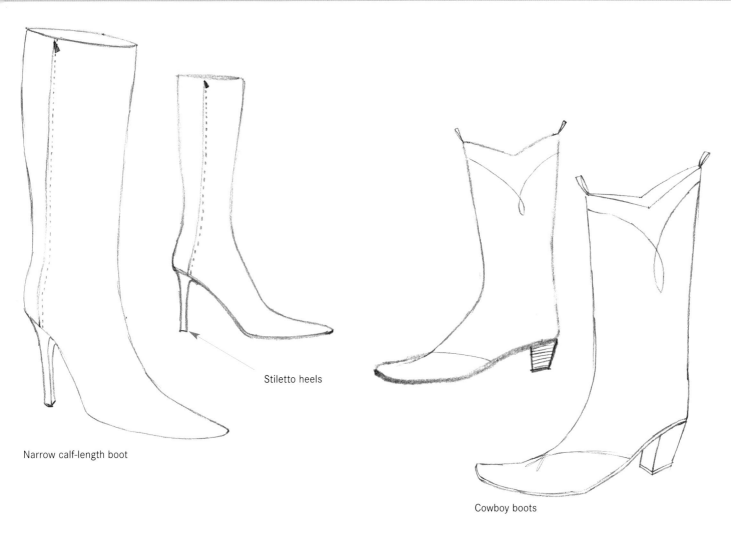

Narrow calf-length boot

Stiletto heels

Cowboy boots

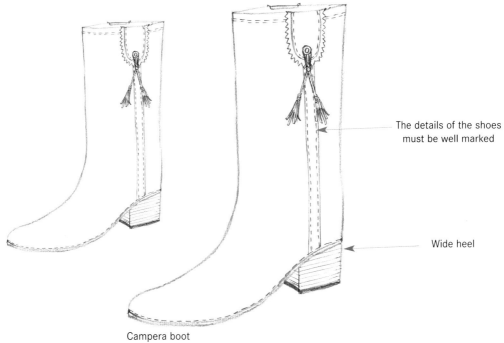

The details of the shoes
must be well marked

Wide heel

Campera boot

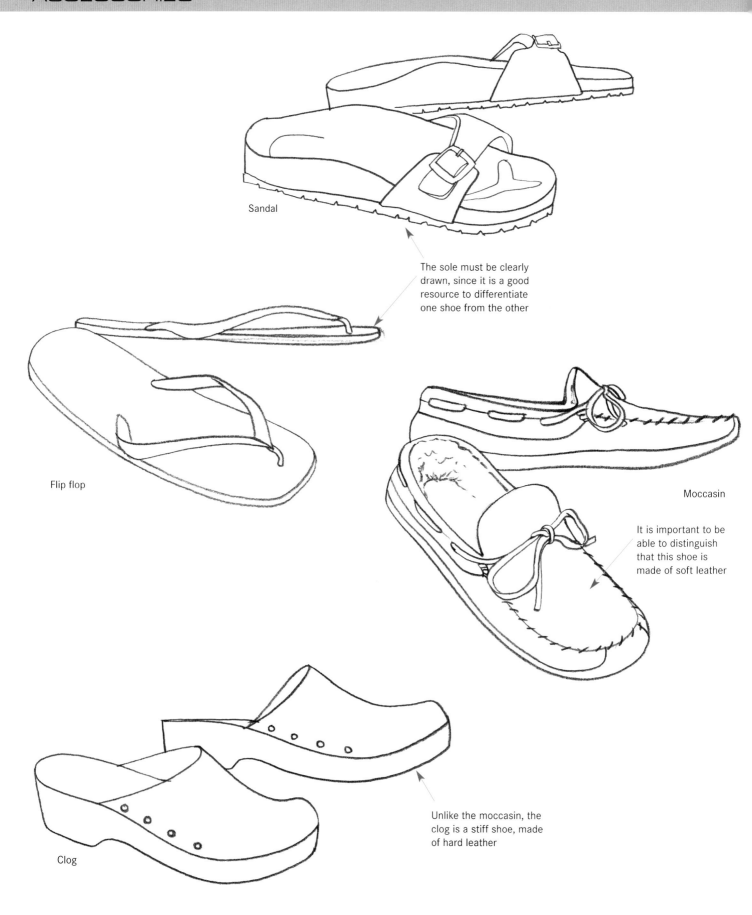

Sandal

The sole must be clearly drawn, since it is a good resource to differentiate one shoe from the other

Flip flop

Moccasin

It is important to be able to distinguish that this shoe is made of soft leather

Clog

Unlike the moccasin, the clog is a stiff shoe, made of hard leather

Sneaker

The laces must be clearly seen

Draw the lockstitches

Canvas shoe

Sneaker with velcro

To shape the padded texture you have to draw an irregular outside profile

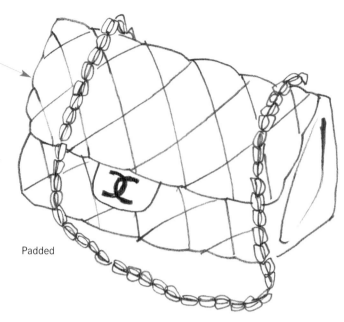

Padded

Classic

Straight lines reflect the rigidity of this piece

Retro

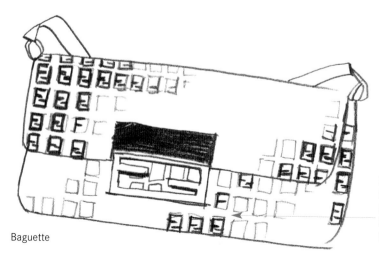

Baguette

It is not necessary to draw all the pattern; it should be diffused from greater to less

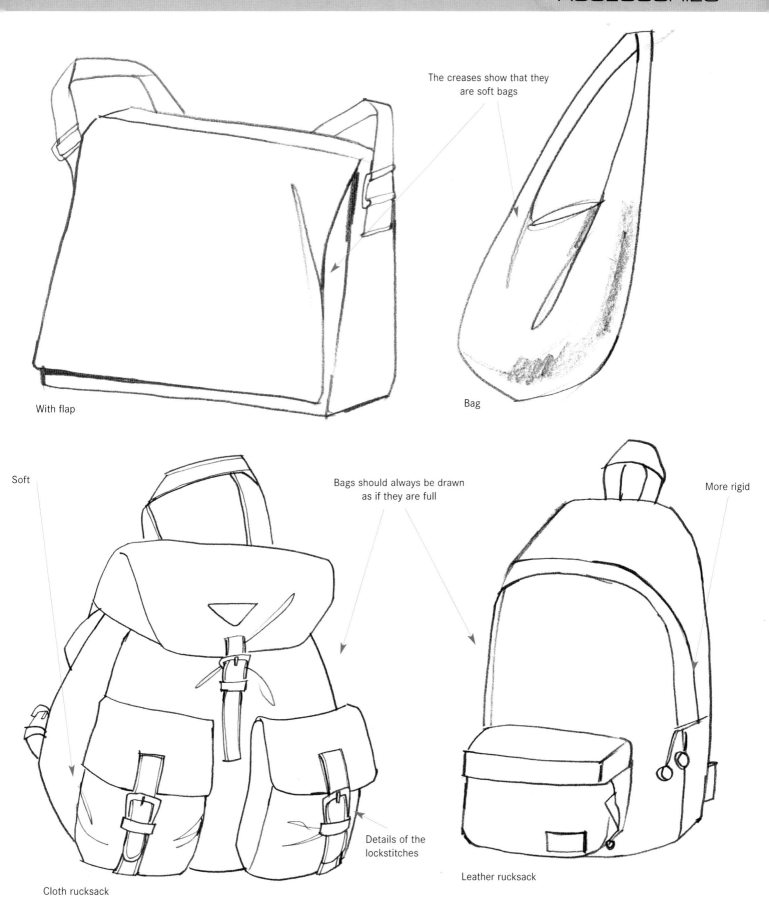

The creases show that they are soft bags

With flap

Bag

Soft

Bags should always be drawn as if they are full

More rigid

Details of the lockstitches

Cloth rucksack

Leather rucksack

ILLUSTRATION
TECHNIQUES

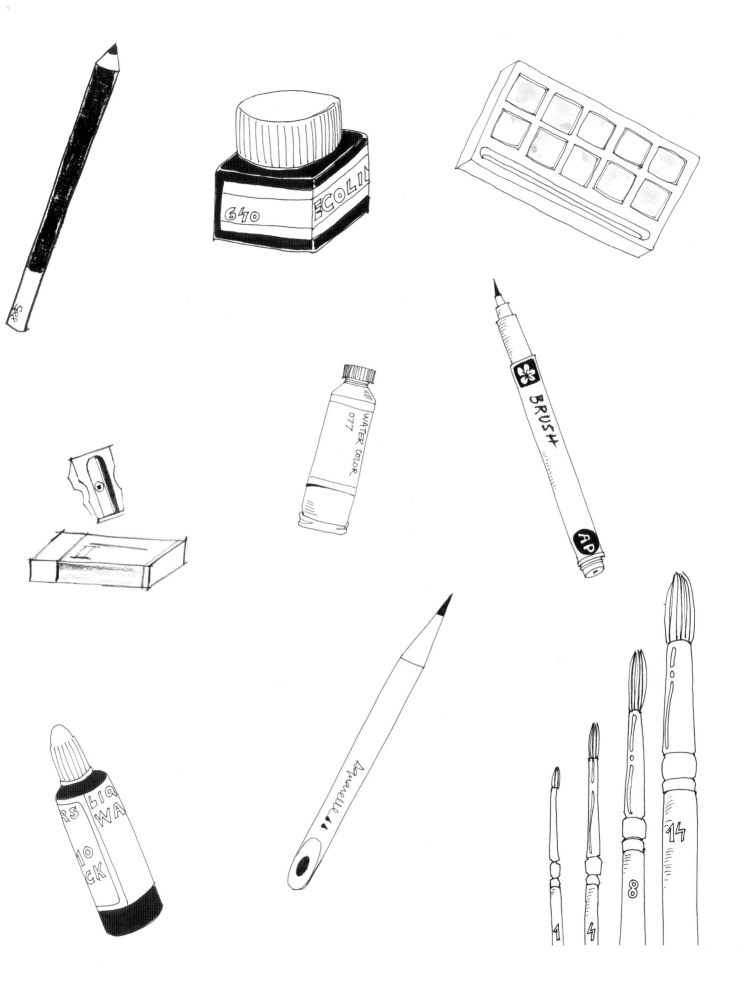

WATERCOLOR

Illustrated with sketches of twenties fashion

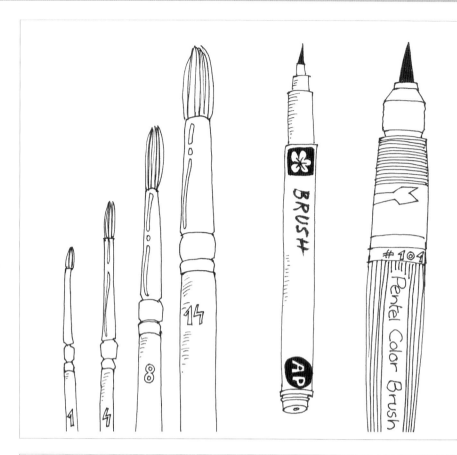

The paper must be thick, especially for watercolor, but without too much texture.

It is better to use good quality brushes; the best are those made from ox ear or camel or marten hair.

For drawings in a single ink, the brush-type markers are the most practical.

There is a wide range of colors for watercolors available; they come in blocks, pencils, anilines, ecolines, tubes, and more.

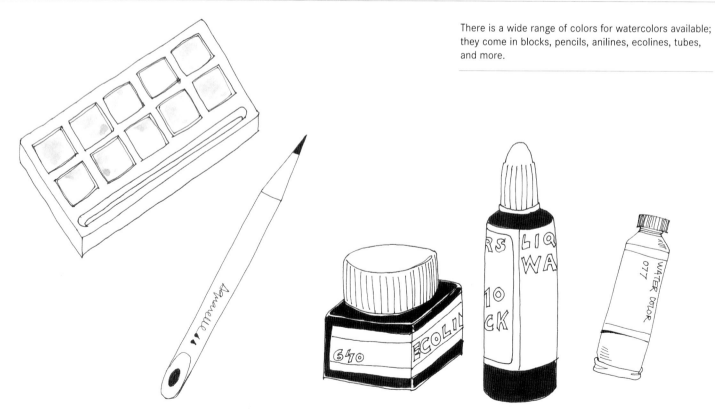

Bear in mind that watercolor dries very quickly, as soon as the water has evaporated.

1. Draw the illustration with a very faint line, so you can rub it out easily.

2. Wet the paper with water.

3. Start by painting the lighter tones; if it is a figure, the lightest tone will be the skin.

4. Now the medium tones, for example the ground of the fabric.

5. Lastly, the darkest and boldest tones; the fabric, shadows, creases, folds.

Watercolors are very useful for coloring illustrations where the design of the fabric is the most relevant – for example, jacquards or prints – as long as they are not particularly detailed. By controlling the amount of water added to the watercolor pencil, the different areas of the fabric's design can be enhanced, as can the folds, shadows, and creases.

For this technique, the pencil is used once the drawing has been colored with watercolors. After the first color sketch, you have to gradually add touches of pencil and finally finish with brushstrokes of watercolor on the shadows, folds, and pattern of the fabric.

Watercolor only

Watercolor with touches of pencil

Finished drawing

After each application and before starting the next, the watercolor must be left to dry. The time it takes depends on the illustration or on the desired effect.

1. Paint the skin.

2. On the areas where the fabric is not in contact with the skin, the tones must be lighter.

3. The opposite is true where the clothes touch the body.

4. Mark the creases and folds.

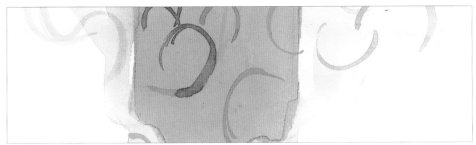

5. The most important thing is to clearly distinguish the different fabric intensities.

The shines of a fabric − whether it be lamé, lurex, or satin − are achieved by leaving blank the areas that show more relief or, depending on the fabric, drawing little white dots that will reflect gleams from the light. This last step should not be done with watercolor or other water-based paints. Use guasch or any other paint that is compact, instead.

To draw fur, mix all the tones from this material; however, you must wait for each tone to dry before adding the next color.

Feathers, when they are of a single color, must be drawn with very dry watercolor, with very little water. If they are multicolor, follow the same procedure as with fur.

The backgrounds are big blotches of color that enrich the illustration.

Black graphite is used to outline or shadow the drawing, and this technique helps to highlight the drawing.

WAX CRAYON

Illustrated with sketches of thirties fashion

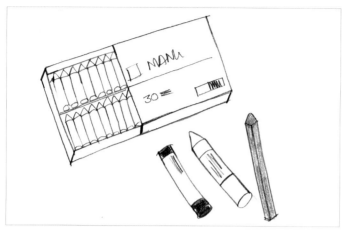

It is recommended to use soft and oily wax crayons, as the hard ones are very difficult to work with.

The work area must be softened by putting newspaper under the sheet, for example. Hard surfaces make it impossible to diffuse or spread the color well.

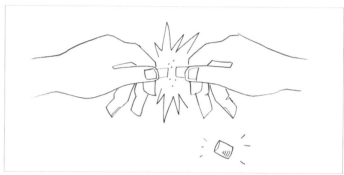

When starting a drawing and after choosing the desired wax crayon, break it in half and choose a wide, short piece to work with.

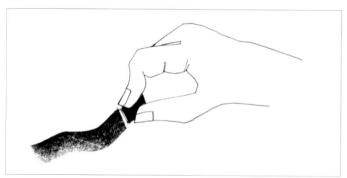

The big surfaces are done with this wide piece, and must be filled as you go with little, short strokes. In this way, the color blends better than with a single long stroke.

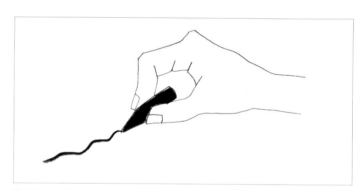

The bits that are sharp should be saved for the thin outlines or for filling in small spaces.

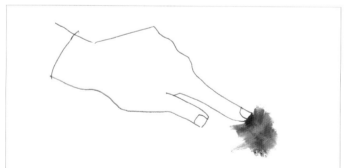

At the end of the drawing, and only at the end, the colors should be blended using the fingers. This process blends the colors and diffuses them, but also creates a hard film that is very difficult to modify.

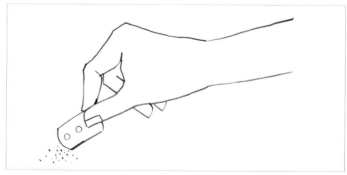

A razor blade or cutter is often used to erase the remains of the wax crayon that may have stayed on the sheet.

2   **3**   **4**

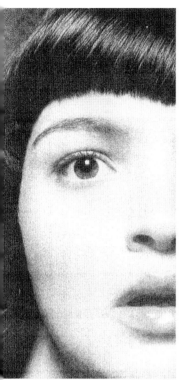 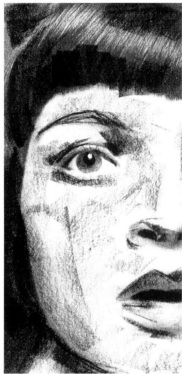  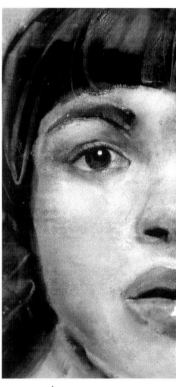

Photocopy a photo on porous (never glossy) paper. It is recommended that it is big, at least 11"x17", because the wax crayons are very oily and need space. The photocopy should be as light as possible.

You must work with the original in front of you, because as you fill the photograph with the wax crayons the image and reference is gradually lost.

Start by coloring the darker areas with black or brown, depending on the photograph.

Never outline a new drawing, this is just a task of filling in. That is the only way to achieve a realist drawing.

White blends the rest of the colors and can be used to erase since it can hide errors.

The entire image must be refilled with wax crayons strokes and not a trace of the photo should be left.

Once the entire sheet is waxed, use fingers to blend all the colors and obtain a more diffused surface. In this process, care must also be taken to cover the pixels of the photocopy.

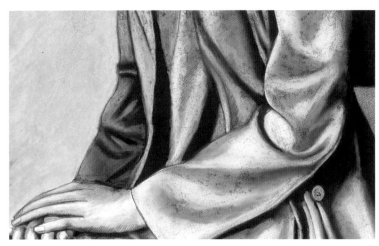

What is most interesting about this technique is that it allows you to do your own photographs and achieve very complete results.

To draw furs, a pencil sketch must be done first. Then fill it with color, changing the tones of the fur and blurring them with white.

To finish, join colors and diffuse them with your fingers, but only in certain areas, as wax crayon drawings look better if there are different textures.

The extremely oily texture of the wax crayons allows you to give, with few strokes, a higher degree of information.

Makeup and hairstyles: Colors with wax crayons mix very well and offer very striking results. For these two sections, work with the most synthesized to the most elaborate. Always draw on large format paper that ventilates the wax crayons.

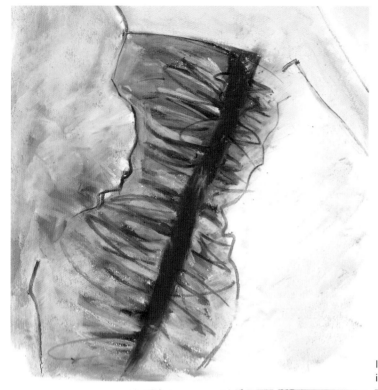

If you work with them and mix them well, wax crayons can achieve very impressive results for fabrics, whether they be silks, wools, or knitted items.

PASTEL

Illustrated with sketches of fifties fashion

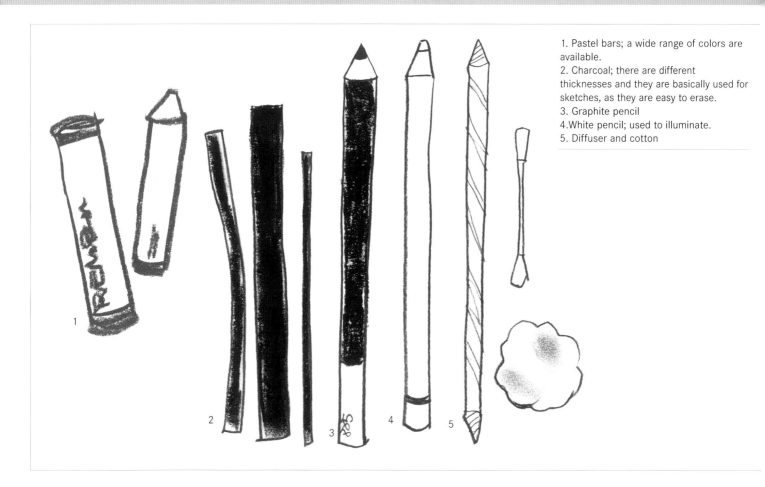

1. Pastel bars; a wide range of colors are available.
2. Charcoal; there are different thicknesses and they are basically used for sketches, as they are easy to erase.
3. Graphite pencil
4. White pencil; used to illuminate.
5. Diffuser and cotton

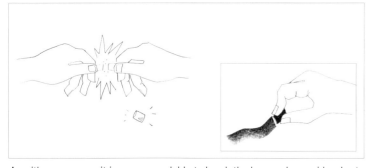

As with wax crayon, it is recommendable to break the bars and use wide, short pieces, as they work better with big areas.

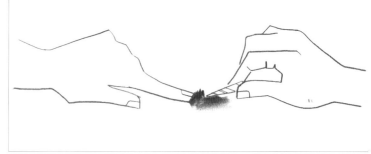

Various methods of bleeding can be used: the diffuser pencil, fingers, or cotton.

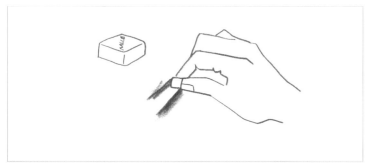

To give shine or shadow, a normal or putty rubber can be used. The white pencil may also be used.

The drawing must be set as soon as it is finished. Pastel, charcoal, and graphite are very dirty materials.

The technique for pastel is very similar to that of wax crayon as long as it is not diffused, since this process makes the texture disappear. The two illustrations show a diffused pastel (1) and one that has not been diffused (2).

Because of its texture and its facility to mix colors, pastel is used a lot in makeup illustrations. Anything from the most discrete diffusion to the most elaborate makeup can be created.

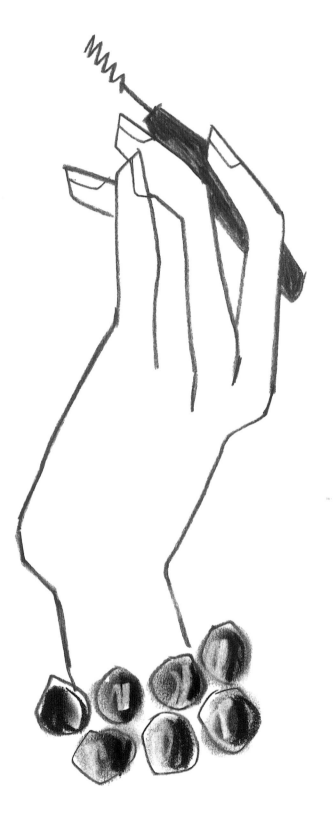

Pastels are ideal for drawing the volume, that is present in certain materials, such as angora, cashmere, and mohair.

Angora

Mohair

Some patterns in diverse drawings that are not very specific, such as smudges, diffuses, and shadows, make good models to work with pastel techniques.

If you work on a surface with a pronounced texture, it will be easy to achieve the appearance of texture.

A granulated or diffused background adds light to the drawing.

Very diffused

MARKER

Illustrated with sketches from seventies fashion

FINE: 0.4 mm

MEDIUM: 1.2 mm

BRUSH

MACRO: 7 mm

Used for very detailed illustrations

FINE: 0.4 mm

If a combination of thicknesses are used, more areas or details can be drawn.

MEDIUM: 1.2 mm

FINE: 0.4 mm

Used for loose drawings of free strokes

MEDIUM: 1.2 mm

These drawings are outlined with a medium thickness and filled in with a very flat ink.

MEDIUM: 1.2 mm

Often used for simple and
synthesized clothing and elements.

BRUSH

Also used for printed transparencies textiles and light fabrics.

BRUSH

First the figures should be drawn in pencil, and then colored in with markers. When the ink has dried, tones can be added to the shadows and folds with the same color used. It is important to make good use of the chromatic ranges. The light tones are reserved for the bottom of the fabric and the skin, while the dark ones are used for shadow. It is recommendable to give the drawing a touch of color pencil at the end.

PENCIL

Illustrated with sketches of 21st-century fashion

1. Color pencils
2. Graphite refill
3. Soft pencil B
4. Hard pencil H
5. Lead pencil
6. Charcoal pencil
7. Eraser and pencil sharpener

Drawn with 1 and 5   Drawn with 3   Drawn with 2 and 6

The hard or H pencil is used for
illustrations with a lot of detail, such
as a seamlock stitch, a pattern, or a
fine ribbing.

The soft or B pencil is used for very
loose drawings with little detail,
where the diverse line thicknesses
have the starring role.

Color pencils must always be soft or B.
They can be applied in two ways, either
on the black pencil of the sketch or
directly onto the sheet.

The charcoal pencil draws an intense black line. Combining it with color makes for a very enriching contrast.

If you want to fill in a large format background, you need to use the pencil with an inclination of 20 degrees to avoid the point leaving marks on the paper and to facilitate the uniformity of the color smudge.

There are various ways to dilute the pencil and preserve the lines:
1. The drawing can be done in charcoal pencil and afterward diluted with a blended colorless marker (illustration on this page).
2. Another way is to draw with a watercolor pencil that will be diluted after with a very light, neutral tone marker or blended marker.

Using the pencil is particularly good for realist drawings.

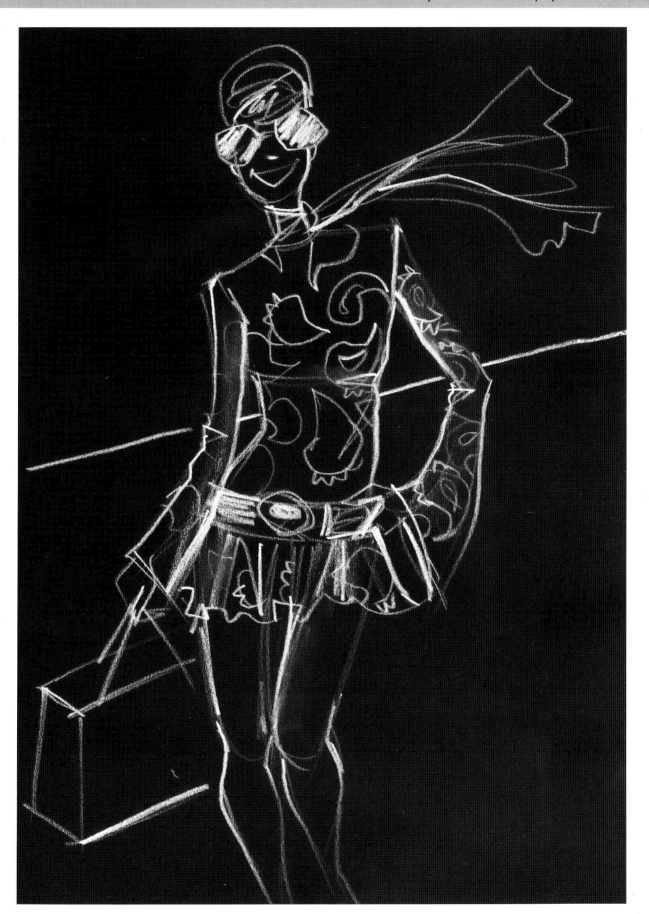

FABRICS

1. The pattern to be drawn must be very carefully studied.

2. It is recommendable to first do a black-and-white sketch on a separate sheet, to familiarize yourself with the drawing.

3. Now the figure can be drawn wearing the garment and the pattern distributed, in black-and-white, without pressing down too much on the pencil.

4. Color the pattern without filling in the whole garment, following at all times the guidelines provided by the light: from dark to light.

The color of the pattern always goes from more intense to less intense. The drawing should not show the whole garment as colored in. It should also be taken into account that the visual of the pencil in a patterned drawing enriches the image.

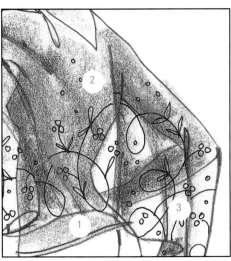

Show the differences in the diverse intensities of color and texture provided by a transparency: firstly the naked skin; then, the parts of the transparent clothing that rest on the skin; and finally the fabric itself draping from the body and hanging lightly in the air.

TWILL

The weaves that form the twill must be studied well to be able to draw them. They should be distributed around the clothing according to the light that falls upon the fabric.

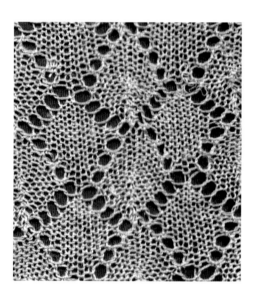

OPENWORK

It is recommendable to draw them abstractly and with very hard pencils or very fine markers, like the 0.4 mm.

BLEND

Very soft or graphite pencils should always be used – as they are easier to diffuse afterwards – to achieve a soft appearence.

Denim is a type of twill with very clear weaves; to create these weaves use a tone that is darker than that of the underlying fabric.

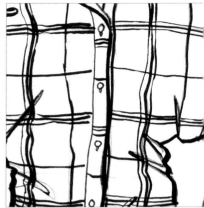

It must be taken into account that the drawing of a pattern is subject to the naturally occurring folds of the fabric. For example, they can not be drawn with straight lines; the creases and folds have to be represented.

The shine is shown leaving
the areas with more relief
and volume white.

1. Skirt with asymmetric cut in viscose circular stitch patterned with polka dots

2. Cotton and net skirt with smocking elastic finish at the hip

3. Compact cotton twill with flounce

4. Irregular ruffles in fabric of silky circular stitching

5. Skirt of denim (hip), satin (bow) and cotton twill (skirt). Pleated flounces with strip put on crossways

6. Flared poplin skirt with cotton dyed lace edging

When there is a flounce or a knot in a pleat,
the lines must appear to be closer
and squeezed together, and more open
as the pleat loses strength.
The bottoms must be drawn irregular.

SYNOPSIS

Compilation of the different techniques through example illustrations
of shoes and legs.

FINE MARKER and
BRUSH MARKER

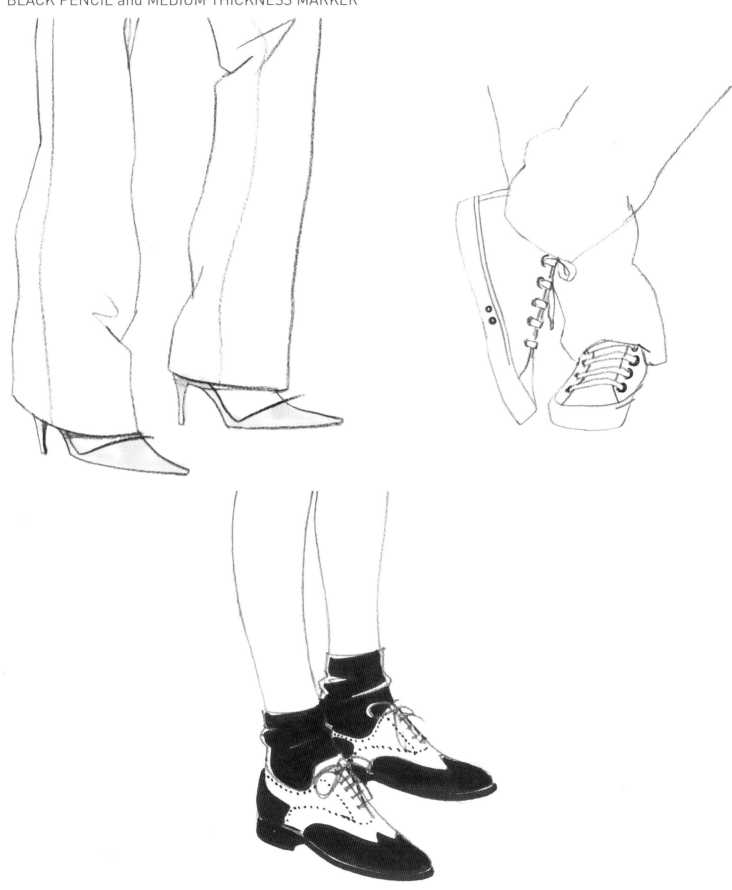

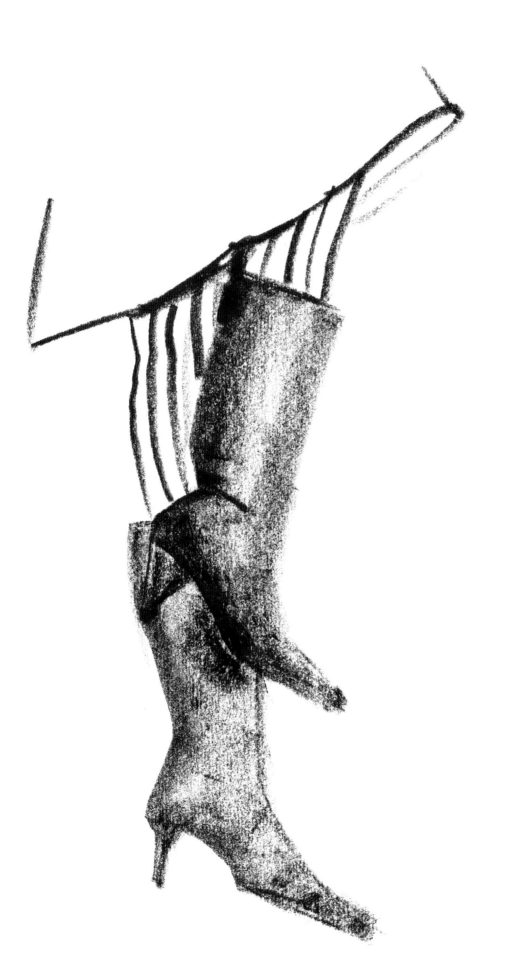

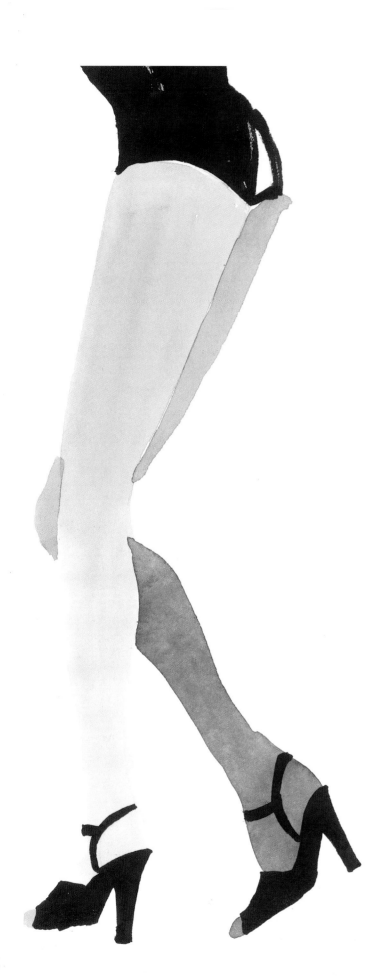
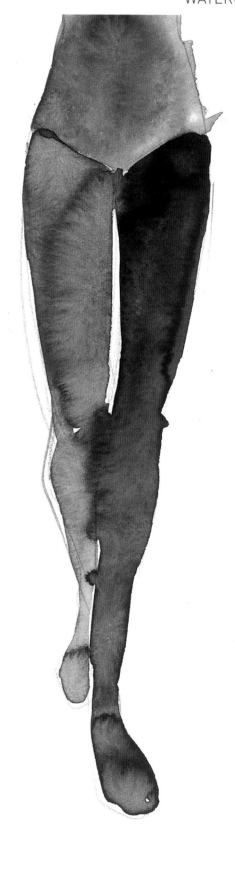